I0620153

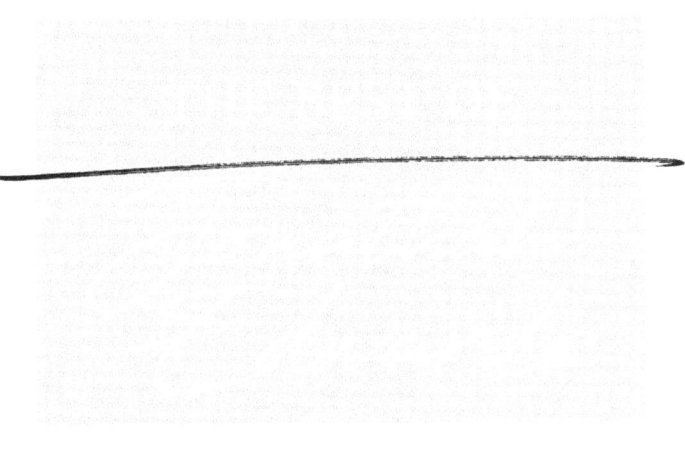

120 Daily Devotions

TO NURTURE YOUR SPIRIT AND
REFRESH YOUR SOUL

Unless otherwise noted, Scripture quotations are taken from the *New King James Version* ®. Copyright ® 1982 by Thomas Nelson, Inc. Used by permission. All rights reserved.

Editor's note: The selections in this book have been "gently modernized" for today's reader. Words, phrases, and sentence structure have been updated for readability and clarity; new chapter headings and Scripture verses have been combined with excerpts from Jonathan Edwards' text. Every effort has been made to preserve the integrity and intent of Edwards' original writings. Reflection questions at the end of each reading have been included to aid in personal exploration and group discussion.

The Best of Jonathan Edwards
ISBN: 979-8-88898-152-8 - *Paperback*
ISBN: 979-8-88898-153-5 - *Hardcover*
ISBN: 979-8-88898-155-9 - *Ebook*

Copyright © 2024 by Honor Books
Racine, WI

Edited and complied by Stephen W. Sorenson.
Cover design by Faille Schmitz.

ABOUT JONATHAN EDWARDS

More Than Fire and Brimstone

Mention the name Jonathan Edwards these days, and you just might receive a cringe from those at all familiar with him. Isn't he the old-time preacher known for his scathing, finger-wagging sermons about the torments of hell and eternal damnation? Didn't he try to convert people by heaping on guilt and shame? He is, after all, the author of the notorious sermon "Sinners in the Hands of an Angry God."

That Edwards has earned the reputation as a preacher of the fear-mongering, guilt-inducing brand is as unfortunate as it is unfair. Those who pigeonhole him as such miss the complete picture of a towering figure of great intellect and influence—and someone who preached God's love and grace more than he did God's wrath and judgment.

Jonathan Edwards (1703-1758) was born into a Puritan evangelical household in East Windsor, Connecticut—what was then frontier country. He was the fifth of eleven children (the only boy) born to the Reverend Timothy and Esther Edwards. Both parents were known to be devout Christians as well as industrious and intellectually bright. Rev. Edwards was a minister who supplemented his income by tutoring local schoolchildren. Jonathan's childhood education immersed him not only in the study of the Bible and Christian thought but also in classics, natural sciences, and ancient languages. By age seven, he had learned Latin, and by twelve he had added Greek and Hebrew to his linguistic repertoire.

Edwards enjoyed nature and as a young boy wrote essays and recorded scientific observations that showed he could have become an outstanding scientist. In fact, his innate intellectual gifts would have enabled him to excel in any number of fields. Strongly influenced by his religious upbringing, though, Edwards set his mind on ministry.

He entered Yale when he was not yet thirteen and graduated four years later at the head of his class. He primarily studied theology and philosophy but showed a broad range of interests. He kept notebooks labeled "The Mind," "Natural Science," "The Scriptures," and "Miscellanies" in which he chronicled his discoveries and ideas. Following graduation, he accepted a call to pastor a small Presbyterian church in New York, where he stayed for a mere eight months until the church ran out of money to pay him. In 1724, he returned to Yale as a tutor and administrator.

In 1727, Edwards was ordained minister at Northampton, Massachusetts, and assistant to his maternal grandfather, Solomon Stoddard. During this year, Edwards married Sarah Pierrepont, whom he had met eight years earlier, when she was just thirteen. Jonathan and Sarah—daughter of one of the founders of Yale—would go on to raise eleven children together.

When Rev. Stoddard died in 1729, Edwards became sole minister of the church, one of the largest and wealthiest in the colony. A few years later, his sermons ignited a remarkable local revival. Historians now recognize Edwards as being instrumental in the initial impulses of what blossomed into the Great Awakening. This movement, which involved the conversion of hundreds of people, gave Edwards the opportunity to hone his theology about salvation and the work of the Holy Spirit. He wrote several challenging and influential books during this time, including *Reality of Spiritual Light* and *A Faithful Narrative of the Surprising Work of God.*

Soon, numerous "spiritual awakenings" appeared elsewhere in New England. The fire of revival spread and led to the Great Awakening of the mid-1730s and '40s. This movement stoked religious fen-or and expanded the church in the decades prior to the nations founding. Many scholars and researchers have shown that Edwards and other leaders of the era helped shape the thinking that led to the Founding Fathers' theories about what an independent America should encompass.

During those years of spiritual resurgence, Edwards became well known nationally and internationally as a powerful revivalist preacher and persuasive writer on a vast array of religious issues. It was in this time that he wrote two of his landmark works, *The Distinguishing Marks of a Work of the Spirit of God* and *A Treatise Concerning Religious Affections.*

Throughout this period of religious revival and cultural transformation, Edwards remained a steadfast pastor, delivering more than twelve hundred sermons to his Northampton congregation. Recognized as a brilliant thinker and beloved by many in his church, Edwards' pastorate was not without contention. In 1744, a misunderstanding about (or perhaps a mishandling of) church discipline involving young people led to years of bickering and backbiting, much of it aimed at Edwards. Then four years later, he angered many of his parishioners when he tried to impose stricter guidelines for those permitted to partake in Communion. His grandfather had adhered to an "all are welcome" policy, which Edwards felt diminished the sacredness of the sacraments and made no distinction between those who professed Christ as Savior and those who didn't. Despite his recognition in the colonies and in Europe—as well as his growing renown as a man of letters— he was overwhelmingly voted out as pastor in 1750.

Edwards moved his large brood to Stockbridge, Massachusetts, a remote settlement at the time. There, he ministered to a small English congregation and served as missionary to Mahican and Mohawk Indians. In this isolated and relatively tranquil setting, he had more time for study and writing. During the years of 1751 to 1757, he wrote many of his most celebrated and enduring works, including *The Freedom of the Will* and *The Nature of True Virtue.*

Despite his "exile" to the frontier outpost, Edwards remained a prominent and revered figure in colonial life. Whatever difficulties he had encountered as the pastor of a local church, he gained renown as a highly influential thinker and writer. Summoned from his missionary post in 1757, Edwards was elected president of Princeton on September 29, five days after the death of his son-in-law Aaron Burr Sr., second president of the college. His tenure as Princeton president proved short-lived (just a few months) but solidified his reputation as a man of erudition. On March 22, 1758, he died following complications from a smallpox inoculation.

George Marsden, author of *Jonathan Edwards: A Life*, succinctly sums up Edwards' legacy: "He was America's greatest theologian, one of America's best philosophers, a famous preacher, a leader in America's early revivals, a missionary, the author of a famous mission biography (of David Brainerd), a virtuoso of spiritual experience, and (with more than a little help from his storied wife, Sarah) the father of 11 children. His most lasting importance is in his dynamic theology of God's ever-present redemptive love and beauty, which can add an exhilarating Natality to the Reformed doctrine of the sovereignty of God."[1]

Adds historian Harry S. Stout: "Edwards the preacher was about far more than fire and brimstone. Yes, hell was a real place in Edwards' mind, and therefore worthy of continual warning to avoid it at all costs. But this was emphatically not the subject that preoccupied his thoughts and visions. Heaven and love were the two most important words in Edwards' sermons and he was far more concerned that his congregation come to a saving knowledge of God through an awareness of the beauty of God's great and powerful redemptive love for them."[2]

Sometimes referred to as "Americas Augustine,"

Edwards' profound insights and influence resonate more than three hundred years after his death.

1. George Marsden, quoted in "Jonathan Edwards at 300," Spark, a publication of Calvin College, www.calvin.edu/publications/spark/2003/winter/edwards.htm.

2. Harry S. Stout, *The New England Soul: Preaching and Religious Culture in Colonial New England*, quoted at www.edwards.yale.edu/about-edwards.

Christ: The Wisdom of God

"We preach Christ crucified, to the Jews a
stumbling block and to the Greeks
foolishness, but to those who are called, both
Jews and Greeks, Christ the power of God
and the wisdom of God."

1 Corinthians 1:23-24

The Corinthian Christians lived in a part of the world where human wisdom was highly valued. As the apostle observed in 1 Corinthians 1:22, "Greeks seek after wisdom." Corinth was not far from Athens, which long had been the most famous seat of philosophy and learning in the world. The apostle therefore observed how the gospel destroyed and rendered obsolete Greek wisdom. By all their wisdom, the learned Grecians and their great philosophers did not know God.

But after they had done their utmost to no effect, it pleased God at length to reveal Himself by the gospel that they considered foolishness. He chose "the foolish things of the world to put to shame the wise" (1 Cor. 1:27). And the apostle informed them in the text why He did this: "that no flesh should glory in His presence" (1 Cor. 1:29). Wisdom was a thing the Greeks admired, but Christ is the true light of the world. Through Him alone true wisdom is imparted to the mind.

Reflection

From where do you
seek wisdom?

How highly do you
value the true
wisdom of Christ?

The Uncertainty of Time

> "Indeed, You have made my days as
> handbreadths, and my age is as nothing
> before You; certainly every man at his best
> state is but vapor."
>
> *Psalm 39:5*

We ought to esteem time as being precious because we are uncertain of its continuance. We know that it is very short, but we don't know how short. We don't know how little of it remains. We are every day uncertain whether that day will be the last or whether we will have the whole day.

If a person had but few provisions laid up for a journey and knew that if his provisions would fail he would die along the way, he would be more focused on his choice of provisions. How much more would many people prize their time if they knew they had but a few months, or a few days, more to live!

Multitudes in the world enjoy health and see no signs of approaching death. Many of them will die next month, or next week; many probably will die tomorrow, and some this night. Yet they know nothing about it, and perhaps think nothing about it, and neither they nor their neighbors can say that they are more likely to be taken out of the world sooner than others.

This teaches us how we ought to prize our time, and how careful we ought to be, that we lose none of it.

Reflection

What is involved in
"prizing your time"?
What changes
might you make in
order to make better
use of your time?

God's Gift of Grace

"For by grace you have been saved through faith, and that not of yourselves; it is the gift of God, not of works, lest anyone should boast."

Ephesians 2:8-9

The redeemed receive all their good from God. God is the author of it—the first cause of it, and the only proper cause. It is God who provided a Savior for us. Jesus Christ is not only of God in His person, as He is the only begotten Son of God, but He is from God. He is the gift of God to us.

It is of God that Christ becomes ours, that we are united to Him. It is of God that we receive faith to be close to Him and have an interest in Him. It is of God that we receive all the benefits Christ has purchased. It is God who pardons, justifies, and delivers us from hell. Into His favor the redeemed are received, when they are justified. So it is God who delivers from the dominion of sin, cleanses us from our filthiness, and changes us from our deformity. It is of God that the redeemed receive all their true excellency, wisdom, and holiness.

The redeemed have all from the grace of God. It was of mere grace that God gave us His only begotten Son. The grace is great in proportion to the excellency of what is given.

Reflection

Ponder how God has shown grace to you and why so many people keep trying to "earn" a relationship with Him.

Thank Him for all that He has done, and is doing, for you.

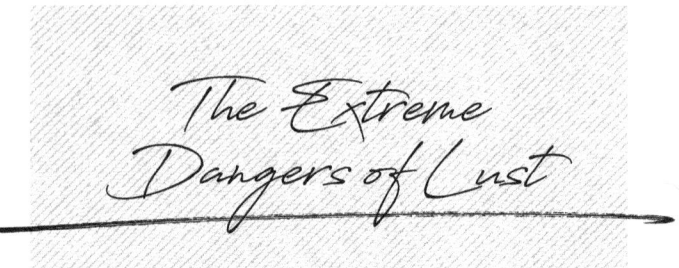

The Extreme Dangers of Lust

"Beloved, I beg you as sojourners and
pilgrims, abstain from fleshly lusts which war
against the soul."

1 Peter 2:11

Sin is deceitful because so far as it prevails and gains the inclination and will, it sways and biases our judgment. So far as any lust prevails, it biases the mind to approve of the lust. So far as any sin sways the inclination or will, so far that sin seems pleasing and prejudices us to think it is right. Thus when any lust has so overtaken a man that it becomes a sinful practice, having gained his will the lust also prejudices his understanding. The more irregularly a man walks, the more his mind probably will be blinded because sin prevails so much more.

Thus many men live in ways that aren't agreeable to the rules of God's Word yet are not aware of it. It is difficult to make them aware because the same lust that leads them into that evil way blinds them in it. Thus if a man pursues a way of malice or envy, the more malice or envy prevails, and the more it will blind his understanding to approve of it. So if a man lives in any way of lasciviousness, the more his impure lust prevails, the more sweet and pleasant will it make the sin appear, and so the more will he be disposed and prejudiced to think there is no evil in it.

Reflection

In what ways have you seen the evidence of these truths in your life?

What can you do to protect yourself against lust?

The Holy Spirit: A Fountain of Holiness and Joy

"Now He who establishes us with you in
Christ and has anointed us is God, who also
has sealed us and given us the Spirit in our
hearts as a guarantee."

2 Corinthians 1:21-22

The saints have both their spiritual excellency and blessedness by the gift of the Holy Spirit and His dwelling in them. They are not only caused by the Holy Spirit but are in Him as their principle. The Holy Spirit becoming an inhabitant is a vital principle in the soul. He, acting in and upon and with the soul, becomes a fountain of true holiness and joy, as a spring is of water by the exertion and diffusion of itself.

John 4:14 states, "Whoever drinks of the water that I shall give him will never thirst. But the water that I shall give him will become in him a fountain of water springing up into everlasting life." Compare this with John 7:38-39: "'He who believes in Me, as the Scripture has said, out of his heart will flow rivers of living water.' But this He spoke concerning the Spirit, whom those believing in Him would receive." It is by partaking of the Holy Spirit that the saints have communion with Christ in His fullness.

Reflection

To what extent are you experiencing the fullness of Christ?

What is involved in "partaking of the Holy Spirit"?

Diligently Avoid Sin

"Therefore let him who thinks he stands take heed lest he fall."

1 Corinthians 10:12

It is quite evident that we ought to use our utmost endeavors to avoid sin, which is inconsistent with needlessly doing those things that expose and lead to sin. And the greater any evil is, the greater care and the more earnest endeavors are required to avoid it. We use proportionately great care to avoid evils that appear to us very great and dreadful. Therefore, the greatest evil of all requires the greatest and utmost care to avoid it.

Sin is an infinite evil because it is committed against an infinitely great and excellent Being, and so is a violation of infinite obligation. Therefore, however great our care is to avoid sin, it cannot be more than proportionate to the evil we would avoid. Our care and endeavor cannot be infinite because the evil of sin is infinite.

We ought to use every method that tends to avoid sin. This is not only reasonable but positively required of us in the Word of God. Joshua 22:5 reads, "Take careful heed to do the commandment and the law which Moses the servant of the Lord commanded you, to love the Lord your God, to walk in all His ways, to keep His commandments, to hold fast to Him, and to serve Him with all your heart and with all your soul." Deuteronomy 4:15-16 reads, "Take careful heed to yourselves . . . lest you act corruptly." Luke 12:15 reads, "Take heed and beware of covetousness." These and many other texts of Scripture plainly require us to use the utmost possible diligence and caution to avoid sin.

Reflection

Which particular sins do you find most alluring?
As you think about your sins, how might you prepare to face them more effectively?

Acknowledge Your Dependence on God

"I cried out to You, O Lord: I said, 'You are
my refuge, my portion in the land of the
living. Attend to my cry.'"

Psalm 142:5-6

Man has the greater occasion and obligation
to acknowledge Gods perfections and all-
sufficiency. The greater the creature's dependence is on God's perfections, the greater occasion
he has to notice them. The greater concern anyone has
with, and is dependent on, the power and grace of God,
the greater occasion he has to notice that power and
grace. The greater and more immediate dependence there
is on divine holiness, the greater occasion there is to
acknowledge that.

We have greater occasion to notice God's all-sufficiency
when all our sufficiency is in every way dependent on
Him. However great and glorious the creature under-
stands God to be, yet if he is not aware of the difference
between God and himself so as to see that God's glory
is great compared with his own, he will not be disposed
to give God the glory due His name. The more men exalt
themselves, the less will they surely be inclined to exalt
God.

Reflection

How is your
dependence on God
influencing your
focus on Him?

How do people exalt
themselves rather
than God?

God's Inevitable Judgment of Wicked Men

> "The Son of Man will send out His angels, and
> they will gather out of His kingdom all things
> that offend, and those who practice lawlessness,
> and will cast them into the furnace of fire.
> There will be wailing and gnashing of teeth."
>
> Matthew 13:41-42

It is no security to wicked men for one moment that there are no visible means of death at hand. It is no security to a natural man that he is now in health and does not see which way he should now immediately go out of the world by any accident, and that there is no visible danger in any respect in his circumstances. The manifold and continual experience of the world in all ages shows there is no evidence that a man is not on the very brink of eternity and that the next step will not be into another world. The unseen ways and means of persons going suddenly out of the world are innumerable and inconceivable. Unconverted men walk over the pit of hell on a rotten covering, and there are innumerable places in this covering so weak that they will not bear their weight, and these places are not seen. The arrows of death fly unseen at noonday; the sharpest sight cannot discern them.

All wicked people's efforts and schemes, which they use to escape hell while they continue to reject Christ and so remain wicked men, do not secure them from hell one moment. Almost every natural man who hears about hell flatters himself that he will escape it; he depends on himself for his own security. He flatters himself in what he has done, in what he is now doing, or in what he intends to do. Everyone lays out matters in his own mind how he will avoid damnation and flatters himself that he contrives well for himself and that his schemes will not fail.

Reflection

Think about people you know who need a personal relationship with Jesus.
What can you do to share His truth and love with them?

Build Your Life on the Right Foundation

"For no other foundation can anyone lay than that which is laid, which is Jesus Christ. Now if anyone builds on this foundation with gold, silver, precious stones, wood, hay, straw, each one's work will become clear; for the Day will declare it, because it will be revealed by fire; and the fire will test each one's work, of what sort it is."

1 Corinthians 3:11–13

All you who never passed under a great change of heart by the mighty power of the Spirit of God on your souls, all you who were never born again and made new creatures and raised from being dead in sin to a state of newness are in the hands of an angry God.

However you may have reformed your life in many things, and may have had religious affections and may keep up a form of religion in your families and closets and in the house of God, it is nothing but His mere pleasure that keeps you from being this moment swallowed up in everlasting destruction. However unconvinced you may now be of the truth of what you hear, by and by you will be fully convinced of it. Those who are gone from being in circumstances similar to yours see that it was so with them because destruction came suddenly upon most of them when they expected nothing of it, while they were saying, "Peace and safety." Now they see that those things on which they depended for peace and safety were nothing but thin air and empty shadows.

Reflection

In what ways does the authors perspective here differ from those that many non-Christians have today?

Why do you think so many people think that their personal "religion" will save them from eternal damnation?

What Account Will You Give to God?

"Each of us shall give account of himself to God."

Romans 14:12

W hen God created you, He created you for an endless duration. He gave you time here in order to prepare for eternity, and your future eternity depends on the improvement of time.

Consider, therefore, what you have done with your past time. You are not now beginning your time. A great deal of time is past and gone; all the wit, power, and treasure of the universe cannot recover it. Many of you may well conclude that more than half of your time is gone. Although you might live to the ordinary age of man, your hourglass is more than half empty, and possibly there are but few sands remaining.

How have you let the precious golden sands of your hourglass run?

Every *day* that you have enjoyed has been precious; yes, your *moments* have been precious. But have you not wasted your precious moments, days—yes, years? If you should count how many days you have lived, what a total would there be! And how precious has every one of those days been! Consider, therefore, what you have done with them.

When you look back, and search, do you not find this past time of your lives in a great measure empty, having not been filled up with any good improvement? And if God, who has given you your time, should now call you to an account, what account could you give Him?

Reflection

How much time do you think is left in your hourglass?

What improvements have you made thus far with the time you've been given?

What improvements can you make in the future?

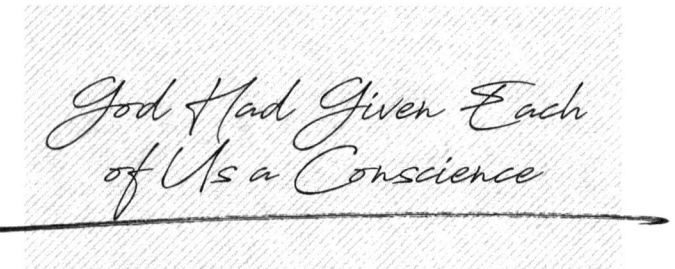

God Had Given Each of Us a Conscience

"Pray for us; for we are confident that we
have a good conscience, in all things desiring
to live honorably."

Hebrews 13:18

Conscience is a principle natural to men, and the work that it does naturally, or of itself, is to give an apprehension of right and wrong and to suggest to the mind the relationship there is between right and wrong and a retribution. The Spirit of God assists conscience to do this work in a further degree than it would do if it were left to itself. He helps it against those things that tend to dull it and obstruct its exercise.

The Spirit of God may indeed act on the mind of a natural man, but He acts in the mind of a saint as an indwelling vital principle. He acts on the mind of an unregenerate person as an extrinsic occasional agent. But He unites Himself with the mind of a saint, takes him for His temple, and actuates and influences him as a new supernatural principle of life and action.

The difference is that the Spirit of God operates in the minds of the godly by uniting Himself to them and living in them, exerting His own nature in the exercise of their faculties.

Reflection

Ask God to reveal
any areas in which
your conscience is
dulled or unclear
and to "exert His
own nature" there.

Religion Is Not Salvation

"Jesus answered and said to him, 'Most assuredly, I say to you, unless one is born again, he cannot see the kingdom of God.'"

John 3:3

A person by mere nature may be prone to be affected by the story of Jesus Christ and the sufferings He underwent, as well as by any other tragic story. A person may be more affected by the story from the interest he conceives mankind to have in it. Yes, he may be affected by it without believing it, as a person may be affected by what he reads in a romance or sees acted in a stage play. He may be affected by a lively and eloquent description of the state of the blessed in heaven, as well as by his imagination being entertained by a romantic description of the pleasantness of fairyland or the like. And a common belief of the truth of such things, from education or otherwise, may help forward their affection.

We read in Scripture about many people who were greatly affected by things of a religious nature, who yet are represented there as being wholly graceless, and many of them very ill. A person therefore may have affecting views of the things of religion and yet be very destitute of spiritual light.

Reflection

What is the difference between feeling "religious" or being affected by religious stories and having the spiritual light that can only come from God through Jesus Christ?

Reflect as You Read the Bible

"The law of the Lord is perfect, converting the soul; the testimony of the Lord is sure, making wise the simple; the statutes of the Lord are right, rejoicing the heart; the commandment of the Lord is pure, enlightening the eyes."

Psalm 19:7-8

J oin self-reflection with reading and hearing the Word of God. When you read or hear, reflect on yourselves as you go along, comparing yourselves and your own ways with what you read or hear. Reflect and consider what agreement or disagreement there is between the Word and your ways. The Scriptures testify against all manner of sin and contain directions for every duty. As the apostle wrote in 2 Timothy 3:16, "All Scripture is given by inspiration of God, and is profitable for doctrine, for reproof, for correction, for instruction in righteousness." Therefore when you read there the rules given us by Christ and His apostles, reflect and consider, each one of you, *Do I live according to this rule? Or do I live in any respect contrary to it?*

When you read in the historical parts of Scripture an account of the sins of which others have been guilty, reflect on yourselves as you go along, and inquire whether you do not in some degree live in the same or like practices. When you read accounts there about how God reproved the sins of other people and executed judgments on them for their sins, examine whether you are guilty of things of the same nature. When you read the examples of Christ, and of the saints recorded in Scripture, inquire whether you live in ways contrary to those examples. When you read there how God commended and rewarded any persons for their virtues and good deeds, inquire whether you perform those duties for which they were commended and rewarded, or whether you live in the contrary sins or vices.

Reflection

Have you ever tried reading the Bible like this?
If so, what happened?
Why is it essential for us to examine the lives of biblical characters?

God's Unique Voice

"'Is not My word like a fire?' says the Lord,
'And like a hammer that breaks the rock in
pieces?'"

Jeremiah 23:29

I f Christ should now appear to anyone as He did
on the mount at His transfiguration, or if He
should appear to the world in His heavenly glory,
as He will do at the day of judgment, without doubt His
glory and majesty would satisfy everyone that He was
a divine person and that religion was true. It would be
a most reasonable and well-grounded conviction, too.

Why might there not be that stamp of divinity, or
divine glory, on the Word of God, on the scheme and
doctrine of the gospel, that may be in like manner distinguishing and as rationally convincing, provided it is
but seen? It is rational to suppose that when God speaks
to the world, there should be something in His Word
vastly different from men's words.

Supposing that God never had spoken to the world,
but we had notice that He was about to reveal Himself
from heaven and speak to us immediately Himself, or
that He would give us a book of His own dictation, after
what manner should we expect that He would speak?
Would it not be rational to suppose that His speech would
be exceedingly different from men's speech, that there

should be such an excellency and sublimity in His Word—such a stamp of wisdom, holiness, majesty, and other divine perfections—that the word of men—yes, of the wisest of men—would appear mean and base in comparison to it? Doubtless it would be thought rational to expect this and unreasonable to think otherwise.

When a wise man speaks in the exercise of his wisdom, something in everything he says is very distinguishable from the talk of a little child. So without doubt, and much more, is the speech of God to be distinguished from that of the wisest men.

Reflection

Consider how much time you spend reading and studying God's Word.

What does this time reveal about your belief in, and commitment to, God and His Word?

Give God the Glory

"Give to the Lord the glory due His name."

Psalm 96:8

L et us be exhorted to exalt God alone and ascribe to Him all the glory of redemption. Let
us obtain and increase our awareness of our
dependence on God, to have our eyes on Him alone, to
mortify a self-dependent and self-righteous disposition.
Man is naturally prone to exalt himself and depend on
his own power or goodness, as though from himself he
must expect happiness.

This doctrine teaches us to exalt God alone—as by
trust and reliance, so by praise. Has anyone hope that he
is converted and sanctified, and that His mind is en-
dowed with true excellency and spiritual beauty? That
his sins are forgiven and he has been received into God's
favor? Exalted to the honor and blessedness of being His
child and an heir of eternal life? Let him give God all the
glory, who alone makes him to differ from the worst of
people in this world or the most miserable of the damned
in hell. Is any person eminent in holiness and abundant
in good works? Let him ascribe all glory to Him whose
workmanship we are, "created in Christ Jesus for good
works" (Eph. 2:10).

Reflection

In what ways might self-dependent and self-righteous attitudes and actions creep or march into your life?

What is involved in giving God the glory He deserves?

The Bride and the Bridegroom

"As the bridegroom rejoices over the bride, so shall your God rejoice over you."

Isaiah 62:5

There are many ministers in the church of Christ, and there may he several pastors of one particular church. But the church has but one husband. All others are rejected and despised in comparison to Him. He is among the sons as the apple tree among the trees of the woods. They all are barren and worthless; He alone is the fruitful tree. Therefore, leaving all others, the church gives herself to Him alone and sits under His shadow with great delight. His fruit is sweet to her taste; she takes up her full and entire rest in Him, desiring no other.

The relationship between a minister and his people will be dissolved, and may be dissolved before death. But the union between Christ and His church will never be dissolved, neither before death nor by death, but will endure throughout eternity.

The mutual joy of Christ and His church is like that of bridegroom and bride, as those whom they have chosen above others for their nearest, most intimate, and ever-lasting friends and companions. The church is Christ's chosen.

Reflection

What is the true
relationship
between Jesus and
His church?

Are you completely
faithful to God,
striving to obey
Him and become
more like Him?

Noah's Call to Obey God

"I will establish My covenant with you; and
you shall go into the ark—you, your sons,
your wife, and your sons' wives with you."

Genesis 6:18

oah's undertaking presented great difficulty,
as it exposed him to the continual reproaches
of his neighbors for 120 years. None of them
believed what he told them about a flood that was about
to drown the world. For a man to undertake such a vast
piece of work, under a notion that it should be the means
of saving him when the world would be destroyed, made
him the continual laughingstock of the world. When he
was about to hire workmen, doubtless everyone laughed
at him. We may suppose that, although the workmen
consented to work for wages, yet they laughed at the
folly of the person who employed them. When the ark
was begun, we may suppose that everyone who passed
by and saw such a huge hulk standing there laughed at
it, calling it "Noah's folly."

During these days, men are with difficulty brought
to do or submit to that which makes them the objects of
the reproach of all their neighbors. Indeed, if while some
people reproach them, others stand by them and honor
them, this will support them. But it is very difficult for
a man to go on in a way wherein he makes himself the

laughingstock of the whole world, and wherein he can find none who do not despise him.

But in such an undertaking as this, Noah, at the divine direction, engaged and went through it, so he and his family might he saved from the common destruction that would shortly come. He began and also made an end: "Noah did according to all that the Lord commanded him" (Gen. 7:5).

Reflection

How obedient are you to what God has called you to do and who He has called you to be?

Are you obedient to God even when other people laugh at you?

The Believer's Primary Business

"One thing I do, forgetting those things
which are behind and reaching forward to
those things which are ahead, I press toward
the goal for the prize of the upward call of
God in Christ Jesus."

Philippians 3:13–14

Although men don't obtain heaven by themselves, they do not go there accidentally or without any intention or endeavors of their own. God, in His Word, has directed men to seek their salvation as they would hope to obtain it. There is a race that is set before them, which they must run, and in that race come off victors in order to win the prize.

They must not make this a secondary business or a thing in which they are negligent and careless, or which they do with a slack hand. It must be their great business, being attended to as their great concern. They must not only seek, but strive; they must do what their hands find to do with their might, as men thoroughly engaged in their minds and influenced and set forward by great desire and strong resolution. They must act as those who see so much of the importance of religion above all other things that everything else must be viewed as an occasional matter, and nothing must stand in competition with its duties. This must be the one thing they do. It must be the business to which they make all other matters give place, and to which they are ready to make other

things a sacrifice. They must be ready to part with pleasures and honor, estate and life, and sell everything so
that they may successfully accomplish this business.

It is required of every man that he not only do something in this business, but that he should devote himself
to it, which implies that he should give up himself to
it—all his dealings and temporal enjoyments. This is the
importance of taking up the cross, of taking Christs yoke
on us and denying ourselves to follow Christ.

Reflection

How devoted are you to
accomplishing God's business—
and not allowing anything else
to hinder you in your spiritual
race?

Diligently Pursue God and His Ways

"Strive to enter through the narrow gate."

Luke 13:24

I t becomes the wisdom of God that things of great value and importance should not be obtained without great labor and diligence. Much human learning and great moral accomplishments are not to be obtained without care and labor. It is wisely so ordered in order to maintain in people a due sense of the value of those things that are excellent. If great things were in common easily obtained, it would have a tendency to cause people to slight and undervalue them. People commonly despise those things that are cheap and that are obtained without difficulty.

Reflection

Why must we "strive" in order to receive God's full blessings through salvation?

Which aspects of your spiritual walk with God are the hardest to maintain? Why?

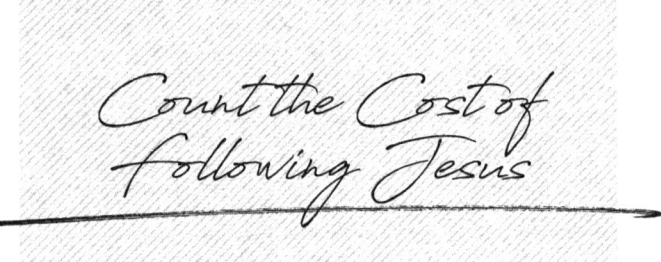

Count the Cost of Following Jesus

"For which of you, intending to build a
tower, doesn't not sit down first and count
the cost, whether he has enough to finish it?"

Luke 14:28

To break completely from all their sins and
give up themselves forever to the business of
religion—without holding onto any lust, sub-
mitting to and complying with every command of God,
and persevering therein—appears to many people so
great a task that they are in vain urged to undertake it.
It seems to them that they would he giving up themselves
to a perpetual bondage.

Although the business of religion is far from really
being as it appears to such men, yet it is indeed a great
undertaking, and it is reasonable that all who are urged
to it should count the cost beforehand and be aware of
the difficulty accompanying it. For though the Devil
discourages many people from this undertaking by rep-
resenting it to be more difficult than it really is, yet with
others he takes a contrary course and flatters them that
it is a very easy thing, a trivial business that may be done
at any time whenever they please, and so emboldens them
to defer it.

Reflection

Why is following
Jesus a great
undertaking?

How devoted are
you to obeying God
completely every
moment of every
day?

Pursue Wise Counsel

"The counsel of the Lord stands forever."

Psalm 33:11

We must never give ourselves any relaxation from this [spiritual] business. It must be continually prosecuted day after day. If sometimes we make a great stir and bustle concerning religion, but then lay all aside to relax, and do so from time to time, it will produce no good effect. We might as well do nothing. The business of religion so followed is not likely to accomplish any good outcome, nor is the work likely to accomplish any good purpose.

It is a business that, by reason of the many difficulties, snares, and dangers that attend it, requires much instruction, consideration, and counsel. There is no business wherein people stand in need of counsel more than in this. It is a difficult undertaking, a hard matter to proceed aright in it. People may take ten thousand wrong ways. There are many labyrinths wherein many unfortunate people are entangled and never find the way out. There are many rocks on which thousands of people have suffered shipwreck, for want of having steered right.

Of themselves, people don't know how to proceed in this business, any more than the Israelites in the wilderness knew where to go without the guidance of the pillar of cloud and fire. There is great need that they search the Scriptures and diligently heed the instructions and directions contained in them, as to a light shining in a dark place, and that they ask counsel of people skilled in these matters. There is no business in which people have so much need of seeking its in seeking God by prayer, for His counsel, that He would lead them in the right way and show them the straight gate.

Reflection

In which specific areas do you need wisdom from God and godly people?
How diligently are you seeking this wisdom?

The Coming Judgment

"Behold, [Jesus] is coming with clouds, and
every eye will see Him, even they who
pierced Him. And all the tribes of the earth
will mourn because of Him."

Revelation 1:7

The inhabitants of the old world would not believe there would come a flood upon the earth as Noah told them, though he told them often. Neither would they take any care to avoid the destruction. Yet such a deluge did come.

So will surely come a more dreadful deluge of divine wrath on this wicked world. We are often forewarned of it in Scripture, and the world, as then, does not believe it. Yet the threatening events will as surely be accomplished as those pronounced against the old world. A day of wrath is coming and will not be delayed one moment beyond its appointed time.

When the floods of wrath come, they will universally overwhelm the wicked world. All who have not taken care will surely be swallowed up in it. The destruction, when it comes, will be infinitely terrible. The destruction of the old world by the flood was terrible, but the coming eternal destruction on the wicked is infinitely more so. That flood of waters was but an image of this awful flood of divine vengeance.

Reflection

How does the truth
of this coming
judgment affect
your desire for
spiritual growth?

The folly of Indecision

"He is a double-minded man, unstable in all his ways."

James 1:8

Many people remain exceedingly undetermined with respect to religion. They are very undetermined in themselves whether to embrace or reject religion. Many who are baptized and make a profession of religion seem to be Christians, yet in their own minds they halt between two opinions. They never fully conclude whether or not to be Christians. They are taught the Christian religion during childhood and have the Bible—the Word preached and the means of grace—all their days. Yet they continue, grow up, and many grow old without resolving whether or not to embrace Christianity. Many remain unresolved as long as they live.

Reflection

Why do so many
people today remain
indecisive about
Jesus and His
claims?

What are some of
the roots of
spiritual indecision?

Time Cannot Be Recovered

"See then that you walk circumspectly, not as fools but as wise, redeeming the time, because the days are evil."

Ephesians 5:15-16

Time is very precious because, when it is past, it cannot be recovered. There are many things that people possess, which if they part with they can obtain again. If a man has parted with something he had, not knowing the worth of it or the need he might have of it, he often can regain it—at least with effort and cost. But it is not so with respect to time. Once time is gone, it is gone forever; no pains, no cost will recover it. Although we repent ever so much that we let it pass, and did not use it well while we had it, it wall mean nothing. Every part of time is successively offered to us, that we may choose whether or not we will make it our own. But there is no delay. It will not wait on us to see whether or not we will comply with the offer. But if we refuse, it is immediately taken away, and never offered again. As to that part of time that is gone, however we have neglected to use it well, it is out of our possession and out of our reach.

Reflection

What happens when
people do not think
about their use of
time?

How might you
better use your time
to benefit the body
of Christ?

A Warning to Backsliders

"His wife looked back behind him, and she
became a pillar of salt."

Genesis 19:26

The only way to seek salvation is to press forward with all your might, and still to look and press forward, never to stand still or slacken your pace. When Lot's wife stopped during her flight and stood still in order to look, her punishment was to stand there forever. She never got any farther.

So often it is with backsliders, although they may live a considerable time afterward. When they look back, after they have been enduring much while seeking salvation, they lose everything. They put themselves under vast disadvantages by quenching the Spirit of God and losing their convictions. They dreadfully harden their hearts and dull their souls. They make way for discouragement, dreadfully strengthen and establish the interest of sin in their hearts, in many ways give Satan great advantages over them, and often provoke God to leave them to hardness of heart. When they look back, their souls presently become dead and hard like the body of Lot's wife. Experience confirms that no people are so difficult to be brought back to repentance as backsliders.

You are still in Sodom, which God is about to destroy

terribly, where you are in danger every minute of having snares, fire, and brimstone come down on your head. Although many have obtained deliverance, you have not.

Considering this should stir you up to escape, and in your escape to press forward—still to press forward—and resolve to press forward forever, no matter what will be in the way, to listen to no temptation, or in any way to slacken or abate your endeavors as long as you live, but if possible to increase in them more and more.

Reflection

What are some ways in which you continue to "look back"? What do you need to let go of? In what areas of your life can you better press forward?

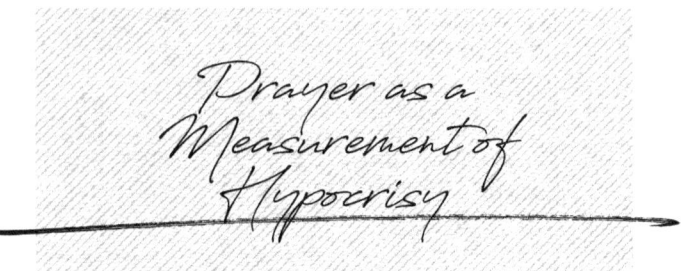

Prayer as a Measurement of Hypocrisy

"Do you not know this of old, since man was
placed on earth, that the triumphing of the
wicked is short, and the joy of the hypocrite
is but for a moment?"

Job 20:4–5

After awhile, hypocrites mostly stop the practice of prayer. We are often taught that hypocrites' seeming goodness and piety is not of a lasting, persevering nature. It is so with respect to their practice of prayer in particular, and especially of secret prayer. They can omit this duty, and its omission is not noticed by other people who know what profession they have made. So, a regard for their reputation does not oblige them still to practice prayer. If others saw how they neglect it, it would exceedingly shock their view of them. But their neglect of prayer does not fall under the observation of many people. Therefore hypocrites may omit this duty and still receive credit for being converted persons.

People of this character can come to neglect secret prayer by degrees without shocking their peace. Indeed, for a converted person to live in a great measure without secret prayer is very wide of the notion the hypocrites once had of a true convert, yet they find ways by degrees to alter their notions and bring their principles to match with their inclinations. At length, hypocrites come to believe that a person may be a convert and yet greatly neglect prayer. In time, they can bring all things to suit well together—a hope of heaven, an indulgence of sloth, gratifying carnal appetites, and living in great measure a prayer-less life. Hypocrites cannot suddenly make these things agree; it must be a work of time, and length of time will bring it to pass. By degrees, they find ways to guard and defend their consciences against those powerful enemies so that those enemies, and a quiet and secure conscience, can at length dwell together.

Reflection

Are all Christians who neglect prayer hypocrites? Why or why not? How is your prayer life, particularly the amount of time you spend "secretly" with God?

Feed Your Imagination with Godly Truths

"Whoever looks at a woman to lust for her
has already committed adultery with her in
his heart."

Matthew 5:28

I t is certainly wrong to feed a lust, even in the imagination. It is quite contrary to the holy rules of God's Word. A man, by gratifying his lusts in his imagination and thoughts, may make his soul in the sight of God to be a space of foul spirits and like a cage of every unclean and hateful bird. Sinful imaginations lead to sinful actions and outward behavior in the end. Lust is always first conceived in the imagination and then brought forth in the outward practice. You may see the progress of it in James 1:15: "Then, when desire has conceived, it gives birth to sin."

Such things are abominable in the sight of a pure and holy God. We are commanded to keep at a great distance from spiritual pollution, "hating even the garment defiled by the flesh" (Jude v. 23).

Reflection

What happens when we do not feed our imaginations with godly things?

Think about a time in your life when this happened—and what resulted.

What is pleasurable about mental lust— and why is it so destructive?

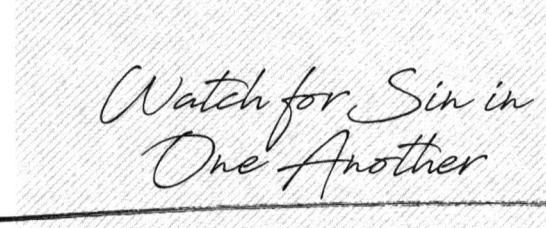

Watch for Sin in One Another

"Confess your trespasses to one another, and pray for one another."

James 5:16

P eople are very apt to bring their principles to their practices and not their practices to their principles, as they ought to do. They, in their practice, do not comply with their consciences; all their strife is about bringing their consciences to comply with their practice.

On account of this deceitfulness of sin and because we have so much sin dwelling in our hearts, it is a difficult thing to pass a true judgment on our own ways and practices. Because of this, we should diligently search and be quite concerned to know if there is some wicked way in us. Hebrews 3:12-13 reads, "Beware, brethren, lest there be in any of you an evil heart of unbelief in departing from the living God; but exhort one another daily, while it is called 'Today,' lest any of you be hardened through the deceitfulness of sin."

Reflection

What is involved in "exhorting one another"?

Why is the church often the last place where people feel free to share their sinfulness and encourage one another to stand firm against sin?

What may be keeping *you* from seeking accountability from other Christians?

True Conversion Leads to Dependence

"I am the vine, you are the branches. He who
abides in Me, and I in him, bears much fruit;
for without Me you can do nothing."

John 15:5

The work of a true convert is not done. He finds a great work to do and great wants to be supplied. He still sees himself to be a poor, empty, helpless creature who still stands in great and continual need of Gods help. He well knows that without God he can do nothing. After a true conversion, the soul is increasingly aware of its own impotence and emptiness. It is still aware of its universal dependence on God for everything.

A true convert is aware that his grace is very imperfect and that he is very far from having all that he desires. Through conversion, new desires are produced in him that he never had before. He now finds within himself holy appetites, a hungering and thirsting after righteousness, a longing after more acquaintance and communion with God. So he still has plenty of business at the throne of grace; in fact, his business there increases rather than diminishes.

Reflection

Would you say that your hunger and thirst for righteousness are increasing or decreasing?

Why?

Are you drawing closer to God, or moving away from Him?

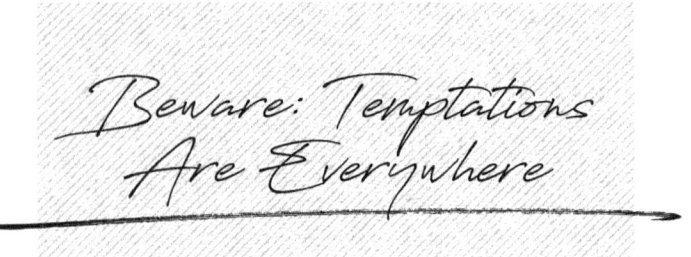

Beware: Temptations Are Everywhere

"As you therefore have received Christ Jesus
the Lord, so walk in Him, rooted and built up
in Him and established in the faith."

Colossians 2:6-7

I f any of us who are parents see our children near the brink of a deep pit, or close by the edge of the precipice of a high mountain, and the ground on which the children stand is slippery and steeply descending directly toward the precipice, would we not consider the children to be at risk? Would we not quickly remove them from their dangerous situation?

The Israelites customarily built their houses with flat roofs, so that persons might walk on the tops of their houses. Therefore God took care to make it a law that all the men should have parapets on the edges of their roofs, lest any person should fall off and be killed. Deuteronomy 22:8 reads, "When you build a new house, then you shall make a parapet for your roof, that you may not bring guilt of bloodshed on your household if anyone falls from it."

Certainly we ought to take similar care not to fall into sin, which carries in it eternal death. We should, as it were, fix a parapet, a guard, to keep us from the edge of the precipice.

Mens lusts are like strong enemies, endeavoring to draw them into sin. If a man stood on a dangerous precipice and enemies were pulling and drawing him, trying to throw him down, would he choose or dare to stand near the edge? Would he consider himself safe if he were close to the edge? Would he not endeavor, for his own safety, to keep at a distance?

Reflection

What kind of "guards" are you using to keep you from sin? From standing too near the edge? How can being "rooted" in Christ help you withstand temptation?

Prayer: A Natural Expression of Faith

"I desire therefore that the men pray
everywhere, lifting up holy hands."

1 Timothy 2:8

W e are abundantly instructed in Scripture that true Christians lead a holy life, that without holiness no man will see the Lord (Heb. 12:14), and that every person who has this hope in Christ purifies himself, even as Christ is pure (1 John 3:3). Proverbs 16:17 reads, "The highway of the upright is to depart from evil." This is the common, beaten road in which all godly people travel.

But how is a life that is in a great measure prayer-less consistent with a holy life? To lead a holy life is to lead a life devoted to God, a life of worshipping and serving Him, a life consecrated to His service. But how does a person lead such a life who does not even maintain the duty of prayer? How can such a person be said to walk by the Spirit and to be a servant of the most high God?

A holy life is a life of faith. The life that true Christians live in the world they live by faith in the Son of God. But who can believe that the person liv es by faith who lives without prayer, which is the natural expression of faith? Prayer is as natural an expression of faith as breathing is of life. To say that a person lives a life of faith and yet lives a prayer-less life is every bit as inconsistent and incredible as to say that a person lives without breathing. A prayer-less life is so far from being holy that it is a profane life. The person who lives such a life lives like a pagan who does not call on God's name. The person who lives a prayer-less life lives without God.

Reflection

How is your prayer life doing? What can you do to improve it?

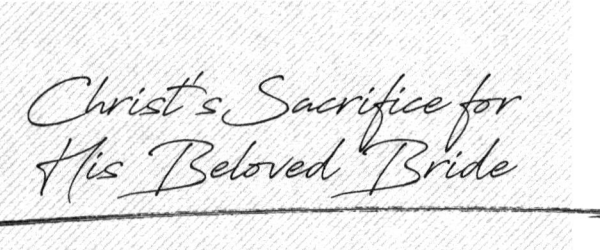

Christ's Sacrifice for His Beloved Bride

"I will rejoice in Jerusalem, and joy in My people."

Isaiah 65:19

We ought to consider how much Christ has done to obtain that joy wherein He rejoices over His church as the bridegroom over the bride. The creation of the world seems to have been to this end, that the eternal Son of God might obtain a spouse toward whom He might pour forth the fountain of love and grace in His heart so God might be glorified.

For the Creator to *make* the creature was a great thing, but for Him to *become* a creature was a greater thing. And He did a much greater thing still in that for this He laid down His life and even suffered death on the cross. He—the Lord of the universe, God over all, blessed forevermore—offered Himself as a sacrifice, in both body and soul, in the flames of divine wrath.

When He offered Himself to God in those extreme labors and sufferings, this was the joy that was set before Him, which made Him cheerfully endure the cross and despise the pain and shame in comparison to this joy.

Reflection

Consider Jesus' sacrifice for you and all humankind so that we may receive salvation and join His beloved church.

How do you think Jesus feels when people continue to reject Him?

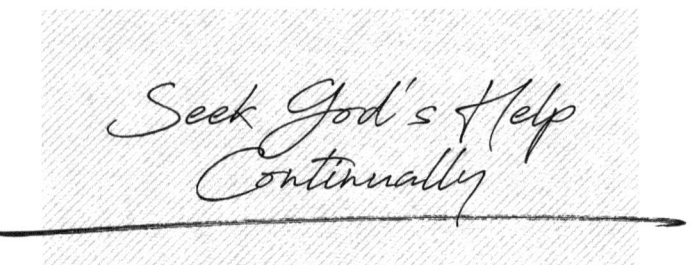

Seek God's Help Continually

"In Him we live and move and have our being."

Acts 17:28

Indeed it is in God we live, move, and have our being. We cannot draw a breath without His help. You need His help every day for the supply of your outward wants, and especially you stand in continual need of Him to help your souls. Without His protection, they would immediately fall into the hands of the Devil, who always stands as a roaring lion, ready, whenever he is permitted, to fall on the souls of men and devour them.

You stand in need of daily supplies from God. Without Him, you can receive no spiritual light or comfort, can exercise no grace, and can bring forth no fruit. Without God, your souls will wither and pine away, and sink into a most wretched state.

You continually need God's instructions and directions. What can a little child do in a vast, howling wilderness without someone to guide and lead the child in the right way? Without God, you will soon fall into snares, pits, and many fatal calamities.

Reflection

To what extent do you seek God's help and acknowledge your dependence on Him?

Do you turn to Him, spreading your needs before Him and offering up your requests to Him?

If not, why not?

Do Not Dull
Your Conscience

"You should no longer walk as the rest of the
Gentiles walk, in the futility of their mind,
having their understanding darkened, being
alienated from the life of God."

Ephesians 4:17-18

The lusts of men's hearts—prejudicing them in favor of sinful practices to which those lusts tend, and in which they delight—stir up carnal reason and cause men, with all the subtlety of which they are capable, to invent pleas and arguments to justify such practices. When men are very strongly inclined and tempted to any wicked practice, and conscience troubles them about it, they will rack their brains to find out arguments to stop the mouth of conscience and make themselves believe that they may lawfully proceed in that practice.

Reflection

What evidences
exist today of
people who justify
sinful practices and
the attitudes behind
them?

Do you do this?

What can you do to
change this
behavior?

Momentary Gratification, Eternal Hell

"So it will be at the end of the age. The angels will come forth, separate the wicked from among the just, and cast them into the furnace of fire. There will be wailing and gnashing of teeth."

Matthew 13:49-50

For the sake of present momentary gratification, the greater part of mankind runs the risk of enduring all these eternal torments. They prefer a small pleasure or little wealth or little earthly honor and greatness that can last but for a moment rather than an escape from eternal punishment. What will it profit a man if he gains the whole world and loses his soul? Or what will a man give in exchange for his soul? What is there in this world that is not a trifle and lighter than vanity in comparison with these eternal things?

How crazy are people when they hear that if they go on in sin they will be eternally miserable, yet they are not moved by it, but hear it with as much carelessness and coldness as if they were in no way concerned with the matter, when they don't know that they may be suffering these torments before the next week ends.

How can people be so careless concerning their eternal and desperate destruction and torment? What a strange stupor and senselessness possesses people's hearts. How common it is to see people, who are told from Sabbath to Sabbath about eternal misery and are as mortal as other people, being so careless about it that they don't seem to be at all restrained by it from whatever their souls lust after. It is not half so much their care to escape eternal misery as it is to get money and land, be influential in the world, and gratify their senses.

Reflection

Why do most people today spend so little time thinking about eternal life?

Ponder how you are living in light of eternity.

On what or whom do you focus most of your attention?

Appropriating God's Peace

"Now may the God of hope fill you with all
joy and peace in believing, that you may
abound in hope by the power of the Holy
Spirit."

Romans 15:13

This peace greatly differs from that which is enjoyed by the men of the world with regard to its exquisite sweetness. This peace is so much above all that natural men enjoy that it surpasses their understanding (Phil. 4:7). It is exquisitely sweet and secure because it has so firm a foundation—the everlasting rock that never can be moved; because it is perfectly agreeable to reason; because it rises from divine principles that are the virtue and proper happiness of men; and because the greatness of the objective good the saints enjoy is no other than the infinite bounty and fullness of God, is the fountain of all good. The fullness of that provision that is made in Christ and the new covenant is a foundation laid for the saints' perfect peace.

Although their peace is not now perfect, that is not due to any defect in the provision made, but to their own imperfection, sin, and darkness. But the more they cling to Christ, and the more they see of the provision made and accept it and cling to that alone, the nearer they are brought to perfect tranquility.

Reflection

How can you appropriate more of God's peace in your life?

How is God's peace different from that experienced by non-Christians?

Strangers in This World

"These all died in faith, not having received the promises, but having seen them afar off were assured of them, embraced them and confessed that they were strangers and pilgrims on the earth."

Hebrews 11:13

Every godly man has his heart in heaven; his affections are mainly set on what is to be obtained there. He focuses on heaven as a traveler who is in a distant land focuses on his own country. The traveler can content himself to be in a strange land for a while, but he prefers his own native land over all others.

The respect a godly person has for heaven may be compared to the respect that a child, when he is abroad, has for his father's house. The child can be contented abroad for a little while, but the place to which he desires to return and dwell is his own home. Heaven is the true saints Fathers house.

The main reason why the godly man has his heart in heaven is because God is there. It is the place where God is gloriously present, where His love is gloriously manifested, where the godly may be with Him, see Him as He is, and love, serve, praise, and enjoy Him perfectly. The believers heart is in heaven because his treasure is there.

Reflection

What difference does the promise of heaven make to you?

How does being a citizen of heaven affect your life here?

What the True Christian Values

"I also count all things loss for the excellence
of the knowledge of Christ Jesus mg Lord,
for whom I have suffered the loss of all
things, and count them as rubbish, that I may
gain Christ."

Philippians 3:8

The saint prefers what he already has of God more than anything in this world. That which was infused into his heart at his conversion is more precious to him than anything that the world can provide. The views that are sometimes given him of the beauty and excellency of God are more precious to him than all the treasures of the wicked. The relationship of a child in which he stands before God, the union that there is between his soul and Jesus Christ, he values more than the greatest earthly dignity. The image of God that is engraved on his soul he values more than any earthly ornaments. It is, in his estimation, better to be adorned with the graces of God's Holy Spirit than to be made to shine in jewels of gold and the most costly pearls, or to be admired for the greatest external beauty. He values the robes of Christs righteousness, which he has on his soul, more than the robes of princes. The spiritual pleasures and delights that he sometimes has in God he prefers far more than all the pleasures of sin.

Reflection

Is this perspective outdated or highly relevant today?

Why?

How does a Christian gain a perspective like this?

Which God Will We Choose?

"I call heaven and earth as witnesses today against you, that I have set before you life and death, blessing and cursing; therefore choose life, that both you and your descendants may live."

Deuteronomy 30:19

A man's choice determines his state. He who chooses God for his portion, and prefers Him above all other things, is a godly man because he chooses and worships Him as God. To respect Him as God is to respect Him above all other things. If any man respects Him as his God, his God He is; there is a union and covenantal relationship between that man and the true God.

Every man is as his god is. If the true God is the One to whom he has a supreme respect, whom he regards above everything else, he is doubtless a servant of the true God. But if the man has something else to which he pays a greater respect than to Jehovah, he is not a godly man.

Inquire, therefore, how it is with you, whether you prefer God above all other things. It may sometimes be difficult for people to determine this to their satisfaction. Ungodly people may be deluded with false affections; godly people in dull frames may be at a loss about it.

When you have occasion to manifest by your practice

which you prefer—when you must either cling to one or the other, and must either forsake other things or forsake God—is it your manner, practically speaking, to prefer God above all other things, even to those earthly things to which your hearts are most wedded?

Reflection

Think about how you spend your resources—time, money, and so on. What do they reveal about your god?
Is there anything or anyone in your life to which or whom you pay greater respect than the God of the Bible?
To which earthly things do you cling most tightly?

God is Completely Holy

"I the Lord, who sanctify you, am holy."

Leviticus 21:8

In that He is God, He is an absolutely and infinitely perfect Being, and it is impossible for Him to do wrong. Because He is eternal and doesn't receive His existence from any other, He cannot be limited in His being, or any attribute, to any certain determinate quantity. If anything has boundaries fixed to it, there must be some cause or reason why those boundaries are fixed just where they are. So it wall follow that every limited thing must have some cause, and therefore the being that has no cause must he unlimited.

It is most evident by the worlds of God that His understanding and power are infinite; He who has made all things out of nothing, and upholds, governs, and manages all things every moment, in all ages, without growing weary, must have infinite power. He must also have infinite knowledge because if He made all things, and upholds and governs all things continually, it will follow that He knows and perfectly sees all things, great and small, in heaven and earth, continually at one view, which cannot he without infinite understanding.

Being thus infinite in understanding and power, He

must also he perfectly holy because unholiness always argues some defect, some blindness. Where there is no darkness or delusion, there can he no unholiness. It is impossible for wickedness to coexist with infinite light. Being infinite in power and knowledge, God must be self-sufficient and all-sufficient. Therefore it is impossible for Him to be under any temptation to do anything wrong, for He can have no end in doing it. When any are tempted to do wrong, it is for selfish ends. But how can an all-sufficient Being, who wants nothing, be tempted to do evil for selfish ends? So, God is completely holy.

Reflection

Why is it important for every believer to seek more understanding concerning Gods character, including His holiness?
How should Gods attributes influence us in our day-to-day lives?

Settled on Scripture's Truth

"Jesus said to him, I am the way, the truth,
and the life. No one comes to the Father
except through Me."

John 14:6

S ome people never come to a settled determination in their minds whether there is any truth
in religion. They hear about things of religion
from childhood but never reach a conclusion in their
minds whether these things are real. Particularly, some
people have never come to any conclusion in their minds
whether there is any such thing as conversion. They hear
much talk about it and know that many people pretend
to be subjects of it, but they never resolve whether everything is merely designed hypocrisy and deception.

Some people never come to any conclusion about
whether the Scriptures are the Word of God and whether
the story concerning Jesus Christ is anything but a fable.
They fear that it is true but sometimes very much doubt
it. Sometimes when they hear arguments for it, they
assent that it is true. But when every little objection or
temptation arises, they call it into question and are always wavering and never settled about it.

Reflection

What conclusions have you reached concerning the gospel message? Concerning the Bible as the Word of God?

What impact do these conclusions make on your daily life?

Why do so many people refuse to make spiritual commitments?

Imitate Christ

"I also imitate Christ."

1 Corinthians 11:1

T he example of no man is set forth in Scripture as our perfect rule, except the example of Christ. We are commanded to follow the examples God set before us, or the acts of the divine nature. Ephesians 5:1 reads, "Therefore be imitators of God as dear children." Matthew 5:48 reads, "Therefore you shall be perfect, just as your Father in heaven is perfect." But the example of Christ Jesus, when on earth, is more especially our pattern.

Christ, though a divine person, was human, as we are human. And He was, in many respects, a partaker of our circumstances. He lived among people. He depended on food, clothing, and such outward supports of life as we do. He was subject to changes of time, afflictions and calamities of this evil world, abuse from men's corruptions, and temptations from Satan, as we are. He was subject to the same law and rule that we are and had many of our trials—and greater trials than we. So, His example is the example that is chiefly offered in Scripture for our imitation.

Reflection

In practical terms, what is involved in "imitating Christ"?

Where do you receive the power to do so?

Resolutely Pursue God and His Ways

"I determined not to know anything among you except Jesus Christ and Him crucified."

1 Corinthians 2:2

Paul did not halt between two opinions or seek with a wavering, unsteady mind, but with full determination and strong resolution. He resolved, by any means possible, that he would attain the resurrection of the dead. He did not say that he was determined to attain it if he could do so by means that were not costly or difficult, or by laboring for it a little time or only now and then, or without any great degree of suffering, or without great loss in his temporal interest. If by any means he could do it, he would, whether the means were easy or difficult. Whether it be a short labor and trial or a long one, whether the cross be light or heavy, it was all one to his resolution. And when it was necessary that he should lose worldly good, or when any great suffering was in his way, it did not cause him to hesitate.

Reflection

How resolute are you in seeking to know God?

Which barriers tend to cause you to waver in faith?

Take Warnings in God's Word Seriously

> "But on this one will I look: on him who is
> poor and of a contrite spirit, and who
> trembles at My word."
>
> *Isaiah 66:2*

J ob was eminently holy, yet avoided sin with the utmost care because he wanted to avoid destruction from God (Job 31). Surely we have as much cause to be cautious, so that we do not expose ourselves to destruction from God. We don't have a greater stock of goodness than Job.

The apostle Paul directed Christians to work out their own salvation with fear and trembling (Phil. 2:12). And the character of a true saint trembles at God's Word, especially at its awful threatenings, as Job did. In contrast, many people today thinking they are converted, disregard the threatenings of God's Word as if they have nothing to do with them, because they suppose they are converted and out of danger. Christ gave His disciples, even those who were converted, as well as others, directions to strive for salvation because broad is the way that leads to destruction, and people are so apt to walk in that way and be damned.

Reflection

As you read the
Bible, how might
you devote more
attention to the
commands and
warnings of God?

God Rewards the Faithful

"Everyone who competes for the prize is temperate in all things. Now they do it to obtain a perishable crown, but we for an imperishable crown."

1 Corinthians 9:25

In those earnest labors that Paul performed, he had respect for the compensation of the reward. He did it for an incorruptible crown. He sought a high degree of glory, because he knew that the more he labored the more he would he rewarded, as appears from what he told the Corinthians: "He who sows sparingly will also reap sparingly, and he who sows bountifully will also reap bountifully" (2 Cor. 9:6). "Each one will receive his own reward according to his own labor" (1 Cor. 3:8).

That Paul had respect for that crown of glory, which his Master had promised, during those great labors and sufferings, is evident from what he wrote to Timothy a little before his death: "I have fought the good fight, I have finished the race, I have kept the faith. Finally, there is laid up for me the crown of righteousness, which the Lord, the righteous Judge, will give to me on that Day, and not to me only but also to all who have loved His appearing" (2 Tim. 4:7-8).

All Christians should follow his example in this also. They should not content themselves with the thought that they have goodness enough to carry them to heaven, but should earnestly seek high degrees of glory. For the higher degrees of glory are promised to extraordinary labors for God.

Reflection

Why do believers often spend so little time thinking about their rewards in heaven?

Ask God to show you any areas of your life in which you are not fully committed to Him, in which you may be "coasting" toward heaven.

Stand Up Boldly for Christ

"I am not ashamed of the gospel of Christ,
for it is the power of God to salvation for
everyone who believes."

Romans 1:16

During Paul's day, almost all those who had prominence in the world—men in honorable stations, men of learning, men of wealth—despised Christianity. They considered it a base, contemptible thing to be a Christian—a follower and worshipper of a poor, crucified man. To be a Christian was regarded as what ruined a man's reputation. Christians were everywhere viewed as fools, derided, and mocked. They were the lowest of mankind, the filth of the world. Thus Christians were greatly tempted to be ashamed of the gospel.

During times when religion is much despised, great men are more ready to be ashamed of it. Many great people seem to think that to appear religious would make them look little. They do not know how to comply with showing a devout spirit, a spirit of supreme love for God, and a strict regard for God's commands. Yet Paul was not ashamed of the gospel of Christ anywhere, or before any person.

When he came to Rome, the metropolis and mistress of the world where the emperor, senators, and chief rulers of the world resided, he was not ashamed of the gospel there. Paul was so far from being ashamed of the crucified Jesus that he gloried in Him above all things. "God forbid that I should boast except in the cross of our Lord Jesus Christ" (Gal. 6:14).

Here is an example for us to follow if at any time we fall in among those who hold religion in contempt, despise us, are ready to deride us for being so precise, and look on us as fools.

Reflection

When people challenge you concerning your faith in Jesus, how do you respond?

Do you boldly proclaim the gospel message, or are you ashamed of it and working hard to hide your Christian faith?

How might God want to use you to boldly share His love and truth?

Guard Your Heart Diligently

"The heart is deceitful above all things, and desperately wicked."

Jeremiah 17:9

M an's heart is a backsliding heart. In it there is a great love and hankering desire after the ease, pleasure, and enjoyments of Sodom, as there was in Lot's wife, by which people are continually vulnerable to temptations to look back. The heart is so inclined toward Sodom that it is difficult to keep the eye from turning that way and the feet from going there.

People also are prone to backsliding through discouragement. The heart is unsteady, soon tired and apt to listen to discouraging temptations. A little difficulty and delay soon overcome its feeble resolutions. Discouragement tends to promote backsliding; it weakens peoples hands, lies as a dead weight on their hearts, and makes them drag heavily. If it continues long, it often fosters senselessness. Convictions are often shaken off that way; they begin first to go off as a result of discouragement.

Backsliding is a disease that is exceedingly secret in its way of working. It is a flattering distemper. It works like a progressive wasting of the body, wherein people often flatter themselves that they are not worse but better, and in a hopeful way toward recovery, until a few days before they die. So backsliding commonly comes on gradually. Backsliders plead that they still are seeking and hope they have not lost their convictions. And by the time they find it out and cannot pretend any longer, they are commonly so far gone that they no longer care if they have lost their convictions.

Maintain the greatest care and diligence to guard your hearts and remain watchful and in constant prayer against backsliding.

Reflection

What are some symptoms of spiritual backsliding?
Do you agree that backsliding often happens gradually and therefore is quite dangerous?
Why or why not?

Despise the Things of the World

"I have coveted no one's silver or gold or apparel."

Acts 20:33

The apostle Paul despised the pleasures of the world. He despised the honors of the world. "Nor did we seek glory from men, either from you or from others" (1 Thess. 2:6). He declared that the world was crucified to him, and he to the world (Gal. 6:14). He didn't seek these things, but the things that were above, that were out of sight of other men. "We do not look at the things which are seen, but at the things which are not seen" (2 Cor. 4:18). He longed greatly after heaven. "We who are in this tent groan, being burdened, not because we want to be unclothed, but further clothed, that mortality may be swallowed up by life" (2 Cor. 5:4).

He considered all men and all things as they related to a spiritual nature, and to another world. In this, the apostle acted as becomes a Christian. For those who are indeed Christians don't belong to this world, and therefore it is very unbecoming in them to have their minds taken up about these things. The example of Paul may make all people ashamed whose minds are occupied chiefly with things of the world, about gaining estates or acquiring honors.

Reflection

In what ways might you strive toward having more indifference toward the world and focus more on the things of heaven?

How might your life be different if you despised the world's pleasures and honors?

Ask God to show you any areas in which you "belong to the world."

True Contentment

"I have learned in whatever state I am, to be content: I know how to be abased, and I know how to abound. Everywhere and in all things I have learned both to be full and to be hungry, both to abound and to suffer need. I can do all things through Christ who strengthens me."

Philippians 4:11-13

Paul went through a great many changes and was almost continually in suffering circumstances, sometimes in one respect, sometimes in another, and sometimes the subject of a great many kinds of suffering together. Yet he had attained such a degree of submission to the will of God as to be contented in every condition and under all circumstances.

What a blessed temperament and disposition of mind was this to which Paul had arrived. And how happy is the person of whom this can now be said truthfully! This person is, as it were, out of the reach of every evil. Nothing can touch him, so as to disturb his rest, because he rests in everything that God orders.

Reflection

Why is it hard sometimes to rest in God no matter what happens?

Which things are particularly difficult for you right now?

How does this reading relate to your situation, or the situation of someone you love?

How Do You Spend Your Time?

"I am already being poured out as a drink offering, and the time of my departure is at hand. I have fought the good fight, I have finished the race, I have kept the faith."

2 Timothy 4:6–7

How great were the pains Paul took in preaching and traveling from place to place over so much of the world, by sea and land, and probably for the most part on foot: instructing and converting the heathen; disputing with gainsayers, heathen Jews, and heretics; strenuously opposing and fighting enemies of the church of Christ; wrestling not with flesh and blood, but against principalities and powers, against the rulers of the darkness of this world, against spiritual wickedness in high places; acting the part of a good soldier, as one who goes to war, putting on Christ and using the whole armor of God; laboring to establish, confirm, and build up saints; reclaiming those who were wandering; delivering those who were ensnared; enlightening the dark; comforting the disconsolate and helping the tempted; rectifying disorders that had happened in churches; exercising ecclesiastical discipline toward offenders and admonishing the saints of the covenant of grace; opening and applying the Scriptures.

We profess to be Christians as did the apostle Paul, and Christ is worthy that we should serve Him as Paul did. But how small are our labors for God, Christ, and our fellow creatures! Although many of us keep ourselves busy, how are our labor and strength spent, and with what is our time filled up? Let us consider ourselves a little, and how we spend our time. We labor to provide for ourselves and families, maintain our reputations, and make our part good among men. But is that all for which we are sent into the world? Did He who made us and gave us our powers of mind and strength of body, and who gives us our time and talents, give them to us chiefly to be spent in this manner, or in serving Him?

Reflection

Consider how you spend your time. How might God want you to use more of your time and talents, mind and body, for His work?
Ask Him to guide you as you evaluate how you spend your time and which things are most worthy of your efforts.

Be Prepared for Opposition

> "The Lord preserves the faithful, and fully repays the proud person. Be of good courage, and He shall strengthen your heart, all you who hope in the Lord."
>
> *Psalm 31:23-24*

The business of religion requires great labor and care. There are many commands to be obeyed and many duties to be done—duties to God, duties to our neighbors, and duties to ourselves.

There is much opposition to accomplishing these duties from without. There is a subtle and powerful adversary placing all manner of roadblocks in the way. There are innumerable temptations of Satan to be resisted and repelled. There is great opposition from the world—innumerable snares laid on every side, many rocks and mountains to be passed over, many streams to be passed through, and many flatteries and enticements from a vain world to be resisted.

There is great opposition from within: a dull and sluggish heart, which is exceedingly averse from that activity in religion that is necessary; a carnal heart, which is averse to religion and spiritual exercises and continually seeking the contrary way; and a proud and a deceitful heart, in which corruption will be exerting itself in all manner of ways. So, nothing can be accomplished with any effect without a most strict and careful watch, great labor, and strife.

Reflection

From which sources does your greatest opposition to spiritual growth come?

How well are you succeeding in spiritual growth in the midst of opposition?

What can you do to become more aware of things that hinder you and your spiritual growth?

Deadly Focus

> "'You shall love the Lord your God with all
> your heart, with all your soul, with all your
> strength, and with all your mind,' and 'your
> neighbor as yourself.'"
>
> *Luke 10:27*

How many plans we make to secure and advance our worldly concerns! Who can count all the schemes that have been formed among us to gain money and honors, and accomplish particular worldly designs? How subtle are we to avoid things that might hurt us in our worldly interest and baffle the designs of people who may be endeavoring to hurt us! But how little is planned concerning the advancement of the church and the good of our neighbors! How many schemes are laid by men to promote their worldly designs, when only one is laid for the advancement of the kingdom of Christ and the good of men! How frequently neighbors meet to determine how they may best advance such and such worldly matters! But how seldom are such meetings held to revive sinking churches, maintain and advance the credit of the gospel, and accomplish charitable designs for the advancement of Christ's kingdom and the comfort and well-being of mankind!

May not these considerations justly be a source of lamentation? How many men are wise in promoting their worldly interests. But what a shame it is that so few show themselves wise as serpents and harmless as doves for Christ! And how commonly it is the reverse of what the apostle advised the Christian Romans: "I want you to be wise in what is good, and simple concerning evil" (Rom. 16:19). Is it not often quite contrary with professing Christians, as it was with the people of Judah and Jerusalem: "They are wise to do evil, but to do good they have no knowledge" (Jer. 4:22)?

Reflection

Do you agree that many Christians spend most of their time and energy on worldly matters?

Why or why not?

What causes this sinful focus to occur?

What can you do to remain focused on loving God, including His church?

The Spirit of Discipleship

"We do not want you to be ignorant,
brethren, of our trouble which came to us in
Asia: that we were burdened beyond measure,
above strength, so that we despaired even of
life."

2 Corinthians 1:8

The apostle Paul willingly endured innumerable and extreme sufferings for the honor of Christ and the good of men. His sufferings were great and occurred more than once or twice. He went through a long series of sufferings that continued from the time of his conversion as long as his life lasted.

Here Christianity appears in its proper colors, to be of such a spirit as Christ so often requires of us, if we would be His disciples. This is to sell all and give to the poor. This is to take up the cross daily and follow Christ. To have such a spirit as this is to have good evidence of being a Christian indeed—a thorough Christian, given to Christ without reserve. And though it is not required of all to endure such great sufferings as Paul did, yet it is required and absolutely necessary that many Christians should be of a spirit to lose all things and suffer all things for Christ, rather than not obey His commands and seek His glory.

Reflection

What kind of sacrifices do you think go along with being a Christian?

To what extent are you willing to suffer for Jesus—in large and small ways?

How might the authors perspectives here influence your view of difficulties?

Called to Bless Other People

> "Blessed is the man who walks not in the counsel of the ungodly, nor stands in the path of sinners . . . But his delight is in the law of the Lord."
>
> *Psalm 1:1–2*

Wherever Paul went, a blessing went with him. He had no silver and gold, but what he imparted to many thousands was worth more to them than if he had bestowed on them the richest jewels. And he not only blessed that generation, but has been blessing, since his death, by the fruits of his lifetime—the foundations he laid and the writings he left for the good of mankind until the worlds end. He then was, and ever since has been, a light to the church next in brightness to the Sun of Righteousness. By means of Paul's excellent spirit and excellent behavior, he became such a blessing.

If we should imitate the apostle in such a spirit and behavior, we also will be made great blessings in the world. We will not live in vain, but will carry a blessing with us wherever we go. Multitudes will be fed with our fruit, and will have reason to praise and bless God for giving us life. How desirable is it to be a blessing! How great was the promise made to Abraham: "In you all the families of the earth shall be blessed" (Gen. 12:3).

Reflection

In what ways are you a blessing to other people?

Why will Christians who live as Paul did certainly bless other people?

Do You Delight in God?

"Trust in the Lord, and do good; dwell in the land, and feed on His faithfulness. Delight yourself also in the Lord, and He shall give you the desires of your heart."

Psalm 37:3-4

I s your conduct consistent with loving God above all? If you do not have a spirit to love Him above your dearest earthly friends and most pleasant earthly enjoyments, the Scriptures plainly state that you are not true Christians. But if you had such a spirit, would you grow weary of the practice of drawing near to Him?

It is the nature of love to be averse to absence and to desire a close access to those whom we love. We love to be with them. We delight to come often to them and have much conversation with them. But when a person who has previously been inclined to converse freely with another by degrees forsakes him, grows strange, and converses with him but little, this plainly shows the coldness of his heart toward the other.

Neglect of prayer seems to be inconsistent with supreme love for God for another reason: It is against the will of God so plainly revealed. True love for God seeks to please Him in everything and universally to conform to His will.

Reflection

What does your prayer life reveal about your love for God and your desire to be in a growing relationship with Him?

Don't Be Afraid; Trust God

"Whenever I am afraid, I will trust in You . . .
In God I have put my trust; I will not fear."

Psalm 56:3–4

People are frequently in distress from fear of temporal evils. We live in an evil world, where we are liable to face an abundance of sorrows and calamities. We spend a great part of our lives in sorrowing for present or past evils, and in fearing future ones. If any person is taken sick and trembles for his life, or if our close friends are at the point of death or in many other dangers, how fearful is our condition!

Now there is a sufficient foundation for peace and safety for those who face such fears and are brought into such dangers. Christ is a refuge in all trouble; there is a foundation for rational support and peace in Him, whatever threatens us. The person whose heart is fixed, trusting in Christ, need not be afraid of any evil tidings.

Reflection

How do you respond when you are afraid?

How can each believer appropriate God's peace and shelter during fearful times?

How do you know God can be trusted?

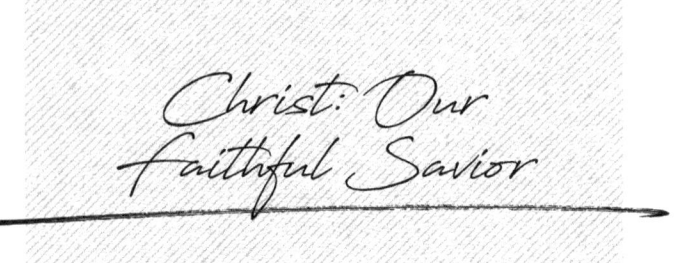

Christ: Our Faithful Savior

"God demonstrates His own love toward us,
in that while we were still sinners, Christ
died for us. Much more then, having now
been justified by His blood, we shall be saved
from wrath through Him."

Romans 5:8–9

It is a fearful condition when one is smitten with a sense of God's dreadful wrath, when he has his heart impressed with the conviction that the great God is not reconciled to him, that He holds him guilty of these and those sins, and that He is angry enough with him to condemn him forever. It is dreadful to lie down and rise up. It is dreadful to eat, drink, and walk about in Gods anger from day to day. A person, in such a situation, is ready to be afraid of everything; he is afraid of meeting God's wrath wherever he goes. He has no peace in his mind. There is a dreadful sound in his ears; his mind is afflicted and tossed with tempest and not comforted, his courage is ready to fail, and his spirit is ready to sink with fear, for how can a poor worm bear the wrath of the great God? What would he not give for peace of conscience. What would he not give if he could find safety!

Christ has undertaken to save all such persons from what they fear, if they come to Him. It is His professional business, the work in which He engaged before the foundation of the world.

People who are in trouble and distressing fear, if they come to Jesus Christ, have this to ease them of their fears: Christ has promised them that He will protect them; that they come on His invitation; that Christ has pledged His faith for their security if they will draw near to Him; and that He is engaged by covenant to God the Father that He will save those afflicted and distressed souls who come to Him.

Reflection

Think about what Jesus is willing to do for every person who comes to Him.

Which persons in your life might God touch through your love and willingness to share Jesus?

Ask Him to guide you to people whose hearts He has prepared to receive Him.

Always Be on Guard

"Watch, stand fast in the faith, be brave, be strong."

1 Corinthians 16:13

L et him who thinks he stands take heed lest lie fall" (1 Cor. 10:12). "Beware, brethren, lest there be in any of you an evil heart of unbelief in departing from the living God; but exhort one another daily, while it is called 'Today,' lest any of you be hardened through the deceitfulness of sin. For we have become partakers of Christ if we hold the beginning of our confidence steadfast to the end" (Heb. 3:12-14).

Thus you see how earnestly the Scriptures press on Christians exhortations to take diligent heed to themselves that they don't fall away. And certainly these cautions are not without reason.

The Scriptures particularly insist on watchfulness in order to persevere in the duty of prayer. "Watch and pray," said Christ, which implies that we should be watchful in our prayers, as the apostle Peter said (1 Peter 4:7). It implies that we should watch against a neglect of prayer as well as against other sins. The apostles so much insisted on watching in order to continue in prayer with all perseverance because there are many temptations to neglect this duty: first, to be inconsistent in it, and from time to time to omit it; then in a great measure to neglect it. The Devil watches by temptation to draw us away from God and hinder us from going to Him in prayer. We are surrounded with one and another tempting object, business, and diversion, and particularly we encounter many things that greatly tempt us to neglect this duty.

Reflection

Which things tempt you not to pray as often, or stop praying altogether?

How do you respond to such temptations?

In what ways has your spiritual growth been hindered or helped as a result of your prayer habits?

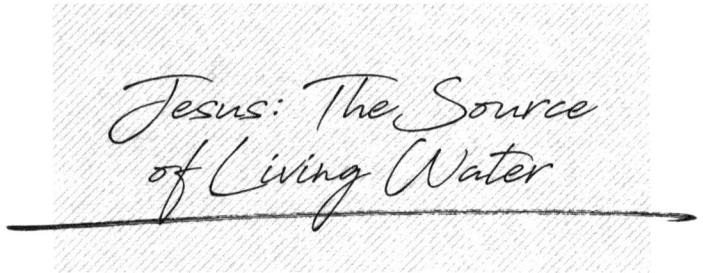

Jesus: The Source
of Living Water

"O God, You are my God; early will I seek
You; my soul thirsts for You . . . in a dry and
thirsty land where there is no water."

Psalm 63:1

Those who travel in such a land, who wander
in such a wilderness, are in extreme need of
water. They are ready to perish for the want
of it, and so they have a great thirst and longing for it.

It is said that Christ is a river of water because there
is such a fullness in Him, so plentiful a provision for the
satisfaction of the needy and longing soul. When a person
is extremely thirsty, a small drink of water will not satisfy him. Yet when he comes to a river, he finds a fullness,
where he may drink full draughts. Christ is like a river
in that He has a sufficiency for one's thirsty soul, and by
supplying him, the fountain is not lessened. There is no
less available for those people who come afterward. A
thirsty man does not sensibly lessen a river by quenching
his thirst.

Christ is like a river in another respect. A river is
continually flowing. Fresh supplies of water come from
the fountainhead continually, so that a man may live near
it and be supplied with water all his life. Likewise, Christ
is an ever-flowing fountain. He is continually supplying
His people, and the fountain is not used up. Those who

live on Christ may receive fresh supplies from Him for all eternity. They may receive an increase of blessedness that is new, and newer still, and that never will come to an end.

Reflection

Are you receiving the spiritual nourishment you need from Christ every day?

Are you abiding in Him, deriving your strength and power from Him and His Spirit?

In which areas are you hurting and thirsty—areas in which Christ can help you if you ask Him?

The Greatest Love

"We love Him because He first loved us."

1 John 4:19

This love of Christ is exceedingly sweet and satisfying from the greatness of it. This love is a dying love; such love was never seen before, and no other love can parallel it. There have been instances of very great love between one earthly friend and another; there was a surpassing love between David and Jonathan. But there never has been such love as Christ has toward believers. The satisfying nature of this love arises also from its sweet fruits. Those precious benefits that Christ bestows on His people, and those precious promises that He has given them, are the fruits of this love. Joy and hope are the constant streams that flow from this fountain, from the love of Christ.

Reflection

Ponder the deep love of Christ—for all people, and for you!

Are you filled with His joy and hope?

If not, why not?

Why are the biblical promises of Christ so precious?

Christ: The Only Way to God

> "Jesus said to him, 'I am the way, the truth,
> and the life. No one comes to the Father
> except through Me.'"
>
> *John 14:6*

We naturally are alienated from God, and God is alienated from us. Our Maker is not at peace with us. But in Christ there is a way for a free communication between God and us, for us to come to God and for God to communicate Himself to us by His Spirit. Christ, by being the way to the Father, is the way to true happiness and contentment. John 10:9 says, "I am the door. If anyone enters by Me, he will be saved, and will go in and out and find pasture."

So, I invite needy, thirsty souls to come to Jesus. You who have not yet come to Christ are in a poor, needy condition. You are in a parched wilderness, in a dry and thirsty land. And if you are thoroughly awakened, you are aware that you are in distress and ready to faint for want of something to satisfy your souls. Come to Christ, who is "as rivers of water in a dry place" (Isa. 32:2). There are abundance and fullness in Him; He is like a river that is always flowing. You may live by that river forever and never be in want.

Through Christ, come to God the Father, from whom you have been separated by sin. He is the way, the truth, and the life; He is the door by which if any man enters he will be saved.

Reflection

Why is this truth,
that Jesus is the
only way to God, so
difficult for many
people to face
today?

What sets this truth
apart from other
"spiritual" truths?

How willing are you
to share this
message with people
you know?

Quiet Rest,
Sweet Refreshment

"Behold, a king will reign in righteousness . .
. As the shadow of a great rock in a weary
land."

Isaiah 32:1-2

There are quiet rest and sweet refreshment in Christ Jesus for those who are weary. He is "as the shadow of a great rock in a weary land."

The comparison used in this text is beautiful and significant. The dry, barren, and scorched wilderness of Arabia is a lively representation of the misery that people have brought on themselves by sin. The wilderness is destitute of any inhabitants except lions, tigers, and fiery serpents. It is barren and parched, without any river or spring. It is a land of drought in which there is seldom any rain, a land exceedingly hot and uncomfortable.

The scorching sunbeams that are ready to consume the spirits of travelers are a fit representation of terror of conscience and the inward sense of God's displeasure. And there being no other shade in which travelers may rest, except only here and there that of a great rock, is a fitting representation of Jesus Christ, who came to redeem us from our misery.

A great rock remains steadfast, unmoved, and unbroken by winds and storms from age to age. Therefore God chose a rock to be an emblem of Christ in the wilderness, when He caused water to issue forth for the children of Israel (Ex. 17:6). The shadow of a great rock is a most fitting representation of the refreshment Jesus Christ gives to weary people.

Reflection

What does the image of the rock reveal to you about Jesus and what He offers every believer?

If you are weary, how might you receive the rest and refreshment He offers you?

What types of barren living do many people experience today?

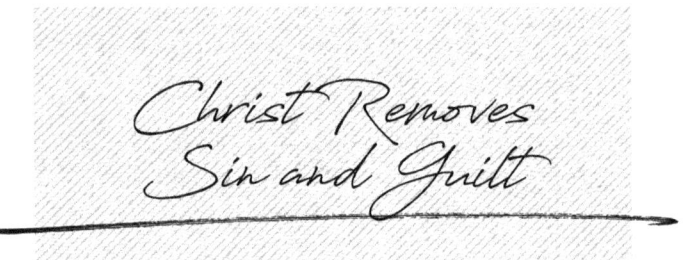

Christ Removes Sin and Guilt

"If we confess our sins, He is faithful and just
to forgive us our sins and to cleanse us from
all unrighteousness."

1 John 1:9

Sin is the most evil and odious tiling, as well as the most mischievous and fatal. It is the most mortal poison. Above all things, it endangers life and the soul, exposes us to the loss of all happiness and the suffering of all misery, and brings Gods wrath. All people have this dreadful evil hanging about them, cleaving firmly to the soul and ruling over it, and keeping it in possession and under absolute command. Sin hangs like a viper onto the heart, or rather holds it as a lion does his prey.

Yet multitudes are unaware of their misery. They are in such a sleep that they are not unquiet in this condition; it is not very burdensome to them. They are so stupefied that they don't know their state, and what is likely to become of them. But other people have their sense so far restored to them that they feel the pain and see the approaching destruction. Sin lies like a heavy' load on their hearts day and night. They cannot put it to rest themselves; it continually oppresses them. It is hound fast to them and is reach to sink them down.

The guilt of such and such great sins is on the soul,

and the man sees no way to get rid of it. He has wearisome days and nights; the guilt makes him ready sometimes to say as the psalmist did, "Oh, that I had wings like a dove! I would fly away and be at rest. Indeed, I would wander far off, and remain in the wilderness. I would hasten my escape from the windy storm and tempest" (Ps. 55:6–8).

But when sinners come to Christ, He takes away that which was their burden—their sin and guilt—that was so heavy on their hearts, that so distressed their minds.

Reflection

Ask God to guide you to anyone in your sphere of influence whose heart and mind He has prepared to hear the gospel message.

Also, reflect on what Jesus has done to enable anyone to receive forgiveness from sin and freedom from guilt.

If your heart and mind are heavy from sin, why not turn to God right now?

A New Creation

"If anyone is in Christ, he is a new creation;
old things have passed away; behold, all
things have become new."

2 Corinthians 5:17

When the sinner comes to Christ, the guilt of sin is at once taken away, and the soul is left free. It is lightened of its burden, delivered from its bondage, and is like a bird escaped from the fowlers snare.

How refreshing is it to the soul to be at once delivered of that which caused so much trouble and terror, to be eased of that which was so burdensome! This is like coming to a cool shade after one has been traveling in a dry and hot wilderness and is almost fainting under the scorching heat. Then Christ also takes away sin itself and mortifies that root of bitterness—which is the cause of all inward tumults and disquietudes in the mind, which make it like the troubled sea that cannot rest—and leaves it all calm. When guilt is taken away and sin is mortified, the foundation of fear, trouble, and pain is removed. The soul is left in peace and serenity.

Christ puts strength and a principle of new life into the weary person who comes to Him. The sinner, before he comes to Christ, is like a sick man who is weakened and brought low, and whose nature is consumed by some strong disease. He is full of pain, so weak that he cannot walk or stand. Therefore, Christ is compared to a physician. "Those who are well have no need of a physician, but those who are sick" (Matt. 9:12). When He comes and speaks the word, He puts a principle of life into the person who was as dead. He gives a principle of spiritual life and the beginning of eternal life. He invigorates the mind with a communication of His life and strength, renews the nature and creates it again, and makes the person a new creation.

Reflection

If you are a believer, think about how Jesus has changed your life and praise Him for all He has done and is doing.
If you are not a believer, reflect on the promises of Jesus and what He desires to do for you.

God's Gift to Every Believer

"Jesus answered and said to her, 'Whoever
drinks of this water will thirst again, but
whoever drinks of the water that I shall give
him will never thirst.'"

John 4:13-14

C hrist gives His Spirit, who calms the mind like
a refreshing breeze of wind. He gives that
strength which lifts the hands that hang down
and strengthens the feeble knees.

Christ gives to those who come to Him such comfort
and pleasure as are enough to make them forget all of
their former labor and travail. A little of true peace, a
little of the joys of the manifested love of Christ, and a
little of the true and holy hope of eternal life are enough
to compensate for all that toil and weariness, and to erase
the remembrance of it from the mind. That peace, which
results from true faith, passes understanding; that joy is
joy unspeakable. There is something peculiarly sweet
and refreshing in this joy that is not in other joys. What
can more effectually encourage the mind, or give a more
rational ground of rejoicing, than a prospect of eternal
glory in the enjoyment of God from Gods own promise
in Christ?

Reflection

How has your relationship with Christ impacted your life or that of people you know?

Do you allow Christ's gifts to permeate your heart and mind so they overflow from your life?

What does the Holy Spirit long to do for you?

Come to the Blessed Jesus

"You will show me the path of life; in Your presence is fullness of joy, at Your right hand are pleasures forevermore."

Psalm 16:11

Christ requires no money to purchase His rest. He invites us to come freely, and for nothing. If we are poor and have no money, we may come. It is His work as Mediator to give rest to the weary; it is the work for which He was anointed, and in which He delights. "The Spirit of the Lord is upon Me, because He has anointed Me to preach the gospel to the poor; He has sent me to heal the brokenhearted, to proclaim liberty to the captives and recovery of sight to the blind, to set at liberty those who are oppressed" (Luke 4:18).

Christ is not only a remedy for your weariness and trouble; He will give you an abundance of the opposite: joy and delight. Those who come to Christ do not only come to a resting place after they have been wandering in a wilderness, they come to a banqueting house where they may rest and feast. They may cease from their former troubles and toils, and enter on a course of delights and spiritual joys.

Christ not only delivers from fears of hell and wrath, but gives hopes of heaven and the enjoyment of God's love. He delivers from inward tumults and inward pain resulting from the guilt of conscience that is like a worm gnawing within. He gives delight and inward glory. He brings us out of a wilderness of pits, drought, and fiery flying spirits and brings us into a pleasant land flowing with milk and honey. He delivers us out of prison, lifts us off the dunghill, sets us among princes, and causes us to inherit the throne of glory.

If anyone is weary, in prison, in captivity, in the wilderness, let him come to the blessed Jesus.

Reflection

What is the "hope of heaven" we can receive through Christ?

How does the joy He provides differ from earthly joy?

Why is it important to remember that Jesus will receive any person who comes to Him?

Jesus: Our Comfort and Strength

"The Lord is my shepherd; I shall not want.
He makes me to lie down in green pastures;
He leads me beside the still waters. He
restores my soul."

Psalm 23:1–3

If a person labors under great bodily weakness or a disease that causes frequent and strong pains, such things will tire out so feeble a creature as man. It may, to such a person, be a comfort and support to remember that he has a Mediator, who knows by experience what pain is, who by His pain has purchased eternal ease and pleasure for him, and who will make his brief sufferings work out a far more exceeding delight, to be bestowed when he will rest from his labors and sorrows.

If a person is brought into great straits such as outward survival, and poverty brings many difficulties and extremities, it may be a supporting and refreshing consideration for such a person to remember that he has a compassionate Savior, who on earth was so poor that He had no place to lay His head, who became poor to make Himself rich, who purchased for him durable riches, and who will make his poverty work out an exceeding and eternal weight of glory.

It is a great comfort to a believer to remember that he has an intercessor with God, that by Him he can have access with confidence to the throne of grace. In Christ, we have so many great and precious promises that all things will work together for good and result in eternal blessedness. God's people, whenever they are scorched by afflictions as by hot sunbeams, may turn to Christ and be adequately sheltered and sweetly refreshed.

Reflection

What does the author challenge us to remember when difficulties arise?

How often do you share with Jesus your pain, and ask for His shelter and refreshment?

What kinds of things hinder you from doing this?

All Things are Under Christ's feet

"The Lord knows how to deliver the godly
out of temptations."

2 Peter 2:9

The Devil, that malicious enemy of God and man, does whatever lies in his power to darken, hinder, and tempt God's people and render their lives uncomfortable. Often he raises needless and groundless worries, casts in doubts, and fills the mind with tormenting fear that tends to hinder God's people exceedingly in the Christian course. The Devil often raises mists and clouds of darkness, and stirs up corruption, and thereby fills the mind with concern and anguish, and sometimes wearies out the soul.

In such a case, if the believers hurry to Jesus Christ, they will find rest in Him. He came into the world to destroy Satan and rescue souls out of his hands. And Christ has all things put under His feet, whether they are things in heaven, earth, or hell. Therefore He can restrain Satan whenever He pleases. Christ is doubtless ready enough to help us under such temptations, we may be assured, because He has been tempted and buffeted by Satan too. Christ is able to help those who are tempted, and He has promised that He will subdue Satan under His people's feet.

Therefore, when Gods people face any of those kinds of weariness, may they turn to Jesus Christ for refuge and rest.

Reflection

How might you face temptations differently from now on?

Why is it so important for us to turn to God for help during temptations?

Looking back on your life so far, what has happened when you have faced strong temptations in your own strength?

Christ: Our Dwelling Place

"Who shall separate us from the love of
Christ?"

Romans 8:35

C hrist has given Himself to be the remedy for
all evil and a fountain of all good, and to be
all things to us that we need. We want clothing, and Christ gives Himself to be our clothing, that we
might put Him on: "For as many of you as were baptized
into Christ have put on Christ" (Gal. 3:27). "Put on the
Lord Jesus Christ" (Rom. 13:14).

We want food, and Christ has given Himself to be
our food. He has given His flesh to be our meat and His
blood to be our drink, to nourish our soul. Thus Christ
tells us that He is the Bread that came down from heaven
and the Bread of Life. Such was Christ's love to us, that
He consented to be slain.

We need a place to live; we by sin have, as it were,
turned ourselves out of house and home. Christ has given
Himself to be the habitation of His people. "Lord, You
have been our dwelling place in all generations" (Ps.
90:1). God's people will dwell in God's temple forever.

Reflection

How has this love
been manifested in
your life?

Have you made
Christ your
dwelling place?

What does that look
like to you?

A Rich Inheritance Awaits Us

"The Spirit Himself bears witness with our
spirit that we are children of God, and if
children, then heirs—heirs of God and joint
heirs with Christ."

Romans 8:16-17

One reason kings are admired is due to their wealth. They have the most precious things laid up in their treasures. We read of the peculiar treasures of kings: "I also gathered for myself silver and gold and the special treasures of kings and of the provinces" (Eccel. 2:8).

But the precious treasures of kings are not to be compared to those precious things that Christ will give His saints in another world: the gold tried in the fire that Christ has purchased with His own blood, those precious jewels, those graces and joys of His Spirit, and that beauty of mind with which He will endow them. King's possessions are very extensive, but these fall short of the extensive possessions of the saints, who possess all things. They are the heirs of God, and all that is God's is theirs so far as it can contribute to their happiness: "He who overcomes shall inherit all things, and I will be his God and he shall be My son" (Rev. 21:7). "Therefore let no one boast in men. For all things are yours" (1 Cor. 3:21).

Reflection

In what ways do believers "possess all things"?

How should what God has in store for believers in heaven relate to our view of earthly riches?

Ponder what an "heir of God" will receive.

Examine Yourself for Sinfulness

"Search me, O God, and know my heart; try
me, and know my anxieties; and see if there
is any wicked way in me, and lead me in the
way everlasting."

Psalm 139:23-24

David was deeply concerned to know this about himself. He searched himself. He examined his heart and ways, but he did not trust that. He was still afraid lest there be some wicked way in him that escaped his notice. Therefore he cried to God to search him. His earnestness appears in the frequent repetition of the same request in different words: "Search me, O God, and know my heart; try me, and know my anxieties."

We ought to be deeply concerned about knowing that we do not live in a *state of sin*. All unregenerate people live in sin. We are born under sin's power and dominion and are sold under sin. Every unconverted sinner is a devoted servant of sin and Satan. We should look on this as having the greatest importance to us, to know in what state we are—whether we have ever had any change made in our hearts from sin to holiness or whether we are still in the gall of bitterness and bondage of iniquity; whether sin was truly mortified in us; whether we live in the sin of unbelief and the rejection of the Savior.

This is what the apostle insisted on with the Corinthians: "Examine yourselves as to whether you are in the faith. Test yourselves. Do you not know yourselves, that Jesus Christ is in you?—unless indeed you are disqualified" (2 Cor. 13:5).

Those who entertain the opinion and hope that they are godly should take great care to ensure that their foundation is right. Those who are in doubt should not give themselves rest until the matter is resolved.

Reflection

What came to mind as you read this?
Why is it important for every believer to compare his or her life to the standards of Gods Word, not just the norms and opinions of other people?

God Hates Sin

"You were once darkness, but now you are light in the Lord. Walk as children of light."

Ephesians 5:8

You once carefully avoided sin. You were watchful to avoid things that were forbidden in God's holy Word. You were careful not to sin by profaning the Sabbath, unsuitably spending time in God's house, or neglecting the duties of reading and prayer. You were careful of your behavior among people, lest you should transgress. If you suspected anything to be sinful then, you dared not do it. But now there is no such care upon your spirit. There is no such watch maintained. You have no such guard on you.

When you are tempted to do or omit anything, the thought does not come with weight on your heart: *Is this sinful or not? Is this contrary to the mind and will of God, or not?* You do not dwell long on such thoughts. You have grown bold and live in sinful neglects and practices that you have light enough to know are sinful. It's as if you think that Christ's disposition with respect to sin has altered, that He is less an enemy to sin now than He was. Instead of being less an enemy to sin than you then thought He was, and instead of being a less dreadful Judge of ungodly men than you imagined or had a sense of in your heart, He is a thousand times more so.

Then, when you were most awakened and convinced, you conceived but little reality. You apprehended imperfectly the enmity of Christs nature against sin and the dreadfulness of His anger against the ungodly. His wrath is infinitely more dreadful than you have yet had any conception of.

Reflection

How sensitive are you to sin?
What causes a Christians sensitivity to sin to erode?
How would you, in discussion with someone, describe the loving Christ who died for humankind and yet hates sin and will judge each person at the final judgment?

Remain faithful to Christ

"[The tribes of Israel] tested and provoked
the Most High God, and did not keep His
testimonies, but turned back and acted
unfaithfully like their fathers."

Psalm 78:56–57

Those who have solemnly vowed to obey Christ in all His commandments as long as they live and have sealed these vows by eating and drinking at the Lords Supper with great solemnity, yet live in ways of sin—or at least do not make it the care of their lives strictly to keep Christs commands—surely such persons render themselves very guilty.

If you find reason to conclude, by a serious and strict examination, that you are one of these people, consider how vile is your treatment of Him who is the same yesterday, today, and forever, and who never is false to any to whom He manifests His favor. How greatly does God complain of such short-lived religion in the Scriptures! "O Ephraim, what shall I do to you? O Judah, what shall I do to you? For your faithfulness is like a morning cloud, and like the early dew it goes away" (Hos. 6:4).

Reflection

Are there any areas of your life in which you are deliberately choosing to pursue sin, disobey Christs commands, and provoke Him?

If so, are you willing to confess your sinfulness and turn away from the sin?

Why or why not?

How do you think God feels when any of His children turn against Him?

A Mandate to Help Those in Need

"Well done, good and faithful servant."

Matthew 25:21

I n the Matthew 25 description of the day of judgment, Christ rehearsed the good works of the saints:

"I was hungry and you gave Me food; I was thirsty and you gave Me drink; I was a stranger and you took Me in; I was naked and you clothed Me; I was sick and you visited Me; I was in prison and you came to Me."

Then the righteous will answer Him, saying, "Lord, when did we see You hungry and feed You, or thirsty and give You drink? When did we see You a stranger and take You in, or naked and clothe You? Or when did we see You sick, or in prison, and come to You?" (Matt. 25:35-39)

Although the saints thought that nothing they had done was worthy to be so accounted of as it was by Christ, yet Christ by His grace esteemed it highly and highly honored them for it, as it here reveals: "The King will answer and say to them, 'Assuredly, I say to you, inasmuch as you did it to one of the least of these My brethren, you did it to Me'" (Matt. 25:40).

Reflection

What do you think is
the main point of
this reading?

What might God be
telling you about
your life and
ministry?

Ask Him to guide
you to someone who
needs practical help
such as food,
clothing, shelter, or a
visit in prison.

Christ Will Forgive Any Sinner

"For Your name's sake, O Lord, pardon my
iniquity, for it is great."

Psalm 25:11

C hrist will not refuse to save the greatest sinners who in a right manner come to God for
mercy. This is His work. It is His business to
be a Savior of sinners. It is the work for which He came
into the world, and therefore He will not object to it. He
did not come to call the righteous, but sinners, to repentance (Matt. 9:13). Sin is the very evil that He came into
the world to remedy; therefore, He will not object to any
person who is very sinful. The more sinful the person is,
the more need he has of Christ. The more sinfulness
people have, the more need they have of being delivered.
"Those who are well have no need of a physician, but
those who are sick" (Matt. 9:12). The physician will not
object to healing a man who comes to him, who stands
in great need of his help. If a physician of compassion
comes among the sick and wounded, surely he will not
refuse to heal those who stand in most need of healing,
if he is able to heal them.

It is the honor of Christ to save the greatest sinners
when they come to Him, just as it is the honor of a
physician to cure the most desperate diseases or wounds.

Reflection

Some Christians
rank sins in terms
of "little ones" and
"big ones."
But how does Jesus
view the worst sins
and sinners?

Burdened by Guilt?

"The one who comes to Me I will by no means cast out."

John 6:37

P ardon is offered and promised to the greatest sinners if they will come properly to God for mercy. The invitations of the gospel are always in universal terms: "Ho! Everyone who thirsts" (Isa. 55:1); "Come to Me, all you who labor and are heavy laden" (Matt. 11:28).

Let us encourage sinners whose consciences are burdened with guilt to go immediately to God through Christ for mercy. The arms of mercy are open to embrace you. You need not be fearful of coming because of your sins, no matter how black they are. If you had as much guilt on your soul as all the wicked people in the world and all the damned souls in hell, if you come to God to receive mercy, seeking pardon only through the free mercy of God in Christ, you would need not be afraid. The greatness of your sins would be no hindrance to your pardon. Therefore, if your soul is burdened, and you are distressed for fear of hell, you need not to bear that burden and distress any longer. If you are willing, you may freely come, unload yourself, cast all your burdens on Christ, and rest in Him.

Reflection

Are you hiding any
secret sins, believing
that they are too
bad for God
through Christ to
forgive?

If so, why not give
your burden to God
right now?

The Believer's Glorious Image

"You have put off the old man with his deeds,
and have put on the new man who is renewed
in knowledge according to the image of Him
who created him."

Colossians 3:9–10

What can render a creature more excellent than to have the very image of the Creator? How blessed a change is that which is wrought in conversion, which brings a person to be in the image of God! For though the image of God in Christians in this world is very imperfect, yet it is real. The image of God is their glory, and it may well be called glory because, imperfect as it is, it renders them glorious in the eyes of the heavenly angels.

Indeed, saints have no excellency as they are in and of themselves. In them, that is, in their flesh, dwells no good thing (Rom. 7:18). They are in themselves poor, guilty, and vile creatures, and see themselves to be so. But they have an excellency and glory in them because Christ dwells in them. The excellency that is in them, though it be but as a spark, yet is something ten thousand times more excellent than any ruby, or the most precious pearl ever found on earth, because it is something divine, something of God.

This holy heavenly spark is put into the soul at conversion, and God maintains it there. All the powers of hell cannot put it out because God will keep it alive, and it will prevail more and more. Though it is but small, it is powerful. It has influence over the heart to govern it, brings forth holy fruits in the life, and will not cease to prevail until it has consumed all the corruption left in the heart.

Reflection

What does "being in the image of God" after conversion mean?

If you are a Christian, what is the "heavenly spark" of God within you seeking to accomplish?

True and Lasting Spiritual Riches

"That you may know what is the hope of His calling, what are the riches of the glory of His inheritance in the saints, and what is the exceeding greatness of His power toward us who believe."

Ephesians 1:18–19

C hristians are the possessors and heirs of something real, substantial, and worthy to be called riches. The things they possess are excellent, more precious than gold and rubies. All the desirable things of this world cannot equal them.

Christians have a fountain of infinite good for their comfort, contentment, and joy because God has given Himself to them to be their portion, and He is a God of infinite glory. There is glory in Him to engage their contemplation forever, without ever being satiated. He is also an infinite fountain of love; God is love, yes, an ocean of love without shore or bottom! The glorious Son of God is theirs, that lovely One who was from all eternity Gods delight, rejoicing always before Him. All His beauty is their portion, His dying love is theirs, His very heart is theirs, and His glory and happiness in heaven are theirs, so far as their capacity will allow them to partake of it. He has promised it to them and has taken possession of it in their name.

The saints have inward riches that they carry with them in their hearts. They are rich in faith. They have

Gods grace in their hearts, which is a most excellent treasure and a good foundation of joy because it is the seed of joy. Light is sown for the righteous, and gladness for the upright in heart. And the seed that is sown in their hearts is Gods grace. That seed, however it lies hidden, will certainly in due time spring up and produce rich fruit. This is the good that God reserves for His friends.

Reflection

What are the true riches of every believer?
How can you appropriate them in your life *today*?

The Joy of Discovering God

"That you, being rooted and grounded in
love, may be able to comprehend with all the
saints what is the width and length and depth
and height—to know the love of Christ
which passes knowledge."

Ephesians 3:17-19

The joy of a Christian does not consist merely in the sense of his own good estate, as some might imagine. There is an excellent, transcendent, soul-satisfying sweetness that sometimes fills the soul in understanding the excellency of God. This sort of joy is evidence of sincerity above any other joy, a more sure evidence than a rejoicing in our own good estate. From the joy that the Christian has in the view of God's glory and excellency, consideration of Gods love for him cannot be excluded.

God is sometimes pleased to manifest His love to the saints. Often, during those times when a Christian has the greatest views of God's excellency, he has also the greatest views of His love. The soul is spiritually sensible of God as being present with it, and as manifesting and communicating Himself. The soul has sweet communion with God, tastes the sweetness of His love, and knows a little about the length, breadth, depth, and height of that love that passes knowledge.

Reflection

List as many
attributes of God as
you can, then spend
time thinking about
God's love for you.

Are you
experiencing the
depth of joy
described in this
reading?

Worldly Pleasures vs. Godly Pleasures

"Lord, lift up the light of Your countenance upon us. You have put gladness in my heart."

Psalm 4:6-7

This pleasure is not a mere shadow, an empty delight, as earthly pleasures are, but it is substantial joy. The pleasures of sin last but a little season. They are like the crackling of thorns under a pot or the blazing meteors of the night, which appear for a moment and then vanish. But this pleasure is like the durable light of the stars or sun.

Worldly pleasures are easily overthrown. A little thing will spoil all the pleasures of a king's court. Hainan, in the midst of all his prosperity and greatness, said, "Yet all this avails me nothing, so long as I see Mordecai the Jew sitting at the king's gate" (Est. 5:13). But the changes of time cannot overthrow joys of the saints. If God lifts up the light of His countenance, this will compose and rejoice the heart under the saddest tidings. Saints joy in affliction. Their enemies cannot overthrow this joy. The Devil and even death itself cannot overthrow it. Often it lives, and is in its greatest height, in the midst of the valley of the shadow of death. How often, during the most tormenting death, have martyrs sung in the midst of the flames and under the hands of their cruel tormentors!

Reflection

When times get
tough, do you still
feel joyful in Christ?
Why or why not?
Why are the
pleasures of God
lasting, in contrast
to the pleasures of
sin?

Believers Need Not Fear Death

"O Death, where is your sting?"

1 Corinthians 15:55

It may seem a mystery to the world that people should be happy in death, which the world considers to be the most terrible of all things, but this is the case of saints. Their happiness is built on a rock that will stand the shock of death. When the storm and floods of death come with their greatest violence, this rock stands firm; neither death nor hell can overthrow it.

The notion of death implies destruction, or perishing, in it, but the godly are not destroyed by death. Death cannot destroy them. As Christ says, they will never perish: "Whoever believes in Him should not perish but have eternal life" (John 3:15). A godly man, when he dies, in no way perishes. There is no end put to his life as a Christian because the spiritual life remains unquenched by death. A wicked man, when he dies, dies indeed, because all the life he has ends; he has no other life but temporal life. But a Christians life is hidden with Christ and safely laid up with Him in heaven.

Therefore death cannot reach the Christian s life because it cannot reach heaven. Death can no more reach the believers life than Christ's life. Christ says, for the comfort of His saints, "I am He who lives, and was dead, and behold, I am alive forevermore. Amen. And I have the keys of Hades and of Death" (Rev. 1:18).

Reflection

Think about the hope of eternal life that all believers share. Do you find it easy or difficult to think about your eternal future? Why?

Death Brings Saints to Christ in Heaven

"To me, to live is Christ, and to die is gain . . .
I am hard-pressed between the two, having a
desire to depart and be with Christ, which is
far better."

Philippians 1:21, 23

This life is a dull, lifeless state. There is but a little spiritual life and a great deal of deadness. There is but a little light and a great deal of darkness. There is but a little sense and a great deal of stupidity and senselessness. But when a godly man dies, all this deadness, darkness, stupidity, and senselessness are gone forever, and he immediately enters a state of perfect life, perfect light, activity, and joyfulness. A man's conversion is compared to a resurrection because then he rises from spiritual death: "And you He made alive, who were dead in trespasses and sins" (Eph. 2:1).

Although spiritual life then begins, yet there are great remains of spiritual death after this and but little life. But when a godly man dies, he rises from all remains of spiritual death and enters a state of perfect life. This body is like a prison to the holy soul; it exceedingly clogs, hinders, and cramps it in its spiritual exercises and comforts. But when a saint dies, the soul is released from this prison, this grave, and enters a state of glorious freedom and happiness. So death is made a servant of the saints, to bring them to Christ in heaven, who is their life.

It is "far better" to depart and be with Christ than to continue here. When the saints are enabled to see their own happiness in death, they are enabled exceedingly to rejoice in the midst of the valley of the shadow of death and triumph joyfully over the king of terrors. To saints, death is always a passage or avenue leading out of a world of vanity, sin, and misery into a world of life, light, and glory.

Reflection

How might this view of death affect how you respond to all the pain of earthly life?
Do you fear death? Why or why not?

Christ's Glorious Return

"Then they will see the Son of Man coming
in the clouds with great power and glory."

Mark 13:26

W hen all the people of the earth wail at the
sight of Christ in the clouds of heaven, and
wicked men everywhere shriek and cry
with terrible amazement, the saints will be filled with
praise and transport. We read that when Christ ascended
into heaven, the disciples stood steadfastly looking on
as He went np. But the saints then on earth will view
Christ with more steadfastness as He descends in His
heavenly and exceeding glory. They will feed and feast
their eyes on this majestic sight, beholding in what
solemn and glorious pomp their own blessed Redeemer
descends.

This sight will put a final end to all sorrow, and the
saints' everlasting joy and glory will commence from it.
The hope of the glorious appearing of the great God,
and our Savior Jesus Christ, is said to be a blessed hope:
"Looking for the blessed hope and glorious appearing of
our great God and Savior Jesus Christ" (Titus 2:13). But
when it comes, it will be a more blessed sight.

Reflection

What comes to mind as you envision the end times?

What do you imagine Christ's return will look like?

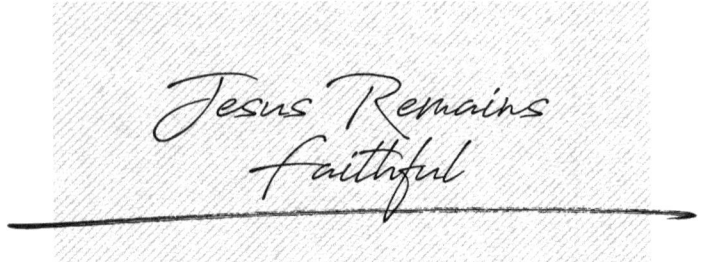

Jesus Remains Faithful

"Jesus Christ is the same yesterday, today, and forever."

Hebrews 13:8

Y ou may greatly comfort yourself that you have an unchangeable friend in Christ Jesus. Faithfulness is rightly viewed as a most necessary and desirable qualification in a friend.

You may learn how excellent His friendship is from His manner of treating His disciples on earth. He graciously treated them as a tender father treats his children, meekly instructing them, most friendly conversing with them, and being ready to pity them, help them, and forgive their infirmities. And then you may consider this doctrine, that He is the same today as He was then, and always will be the same.

Reflection

Think about who Jesus is, and how He longs to love you each day.

How might you apply what the New Testament reveals about Jesus to your daily relationship with Him?

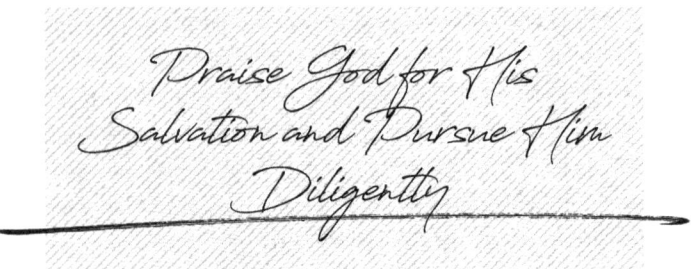

Praise God for His Salvation and Pursue Him Diligently

"Oh come, let us sing to the Lord!"

Psalm 95:1

We came into the world wretched, miserable, and undone creatures, in cruel bondage to sin and Satan, under guilt and under wrath, hostile toward God—the fountain of blessedness— and in a state of condemnation leading to everlasting destruction. But when a man is converted, he is brought out of that state of woe and misery into a sure title to glory, honor, and peace forever. When once a man is converted, all this blessedness that we have heard of is his; he has an absolute right to it. God's work is accomplished for it; His faithful promise is given.

What cause saints have to bless, praise, and extol God's name when they consider the situation they were once in and what a happy state they are now in, for bringing them out of that miserable state into so glorious a state is due only to His free and sovereign grace. "Who makes you differ from another? And what do you have that you did not receive? Now if you did indeed receive it, why do you boast as if you had not received it?" (1 Cor. 4:7).

Thus we may learn the folly of those who are cold

and slack in seeking salvation, seeing that the glory and happiness of Christians is so exceedingly great. How unreasonable it is to expect to obtain that which is so great without effort! With great and indefatigable labor and diligence, men will seek worldly riches and honors that are worth so little, cannot make them happy, and will soon vanish away. Will men expect to obtain such eternal glory and blessedness by seeking it in a slack and cold way?

Reflection

How often do you praise God for what He has done for you? If Jesus were sitting across from you today, what might He say about your commitment to Him—to knowing Him, to sharing His good news with other people, to laboring for His kingdom?

Avoid Anything Leading to Evil

"He who wafts righteously and speaks uprightly, he who despises the gain of oppressions, who gestures with his hands, refusing bribes, who stops his ears from hearing of bloodshed, and shuts his eyes from seeing evil: He will dwell on high."

Isaiah 33:15-16

I t is evident that we ought not only to avoid sin, but things that expose and lead to sin because this is the way we act toward things that pertain to our temporal interest. People avoid not only things that in themselves will hurt or ruin their temporal interest, but also things that tend or expose them to it.

They are careful not to pass rivers and deep waters on rotten ice, although they certainly don't know that they will fall through and drown. They will not only avoid things that would in themselves ruin their estates—such as setting their own houses on fire and burning them up with their possessions, throwing their money into the sea—but they carefully avoid things by which their estates are exposed. They have their eyes about themselves—are careful with whom they deal, are watchful that they are not taken advantage of in their dealings and that they don't make themselves vulnerable to villains and fraudulent persons.

A man sick with a dangerous illness carefully avoids everything that tends to increase the disorder, not only what he knows will cause death but other things that he fears may harm him. Men are in this way inclined to take care of their temporal interests. Therefore, if we are not as careful to avoid sin as we are to avoid injury in our temporal interests, it will show an unmindful disposition toward sin and duty or that we don't much care if we sin against God. God's glory is surely of as much importance and concern as our temporal interest. Certainly we should be as careful not to be exposed to sin against the Majesty of heaven and earth as men are prone to be about a few dollars.

Reflection

Are you more mindful of earthly details than you are of sin?
Why do you think the author mentioned God's glory here?

"Why Doesn't God Comfort Me More?"

> "How long, O Lord? Will You forget me
> forever? How long will You hide Your face
> from me? How long shall I take counsel in
> my soul, having sorrow in my heart daily?"
>
> Psalm 13:1-2

S ome godly persons are the subjects of great outward afflictions and great spiritual darkness. Some truly godly persons spend great parts of their lives in the dark—in exercising doubts, anxious thoughts, and distressing fears. And often God's people argue that if God loved them, and had made them His children, He would never leave them in such darkness and distress. He would give them more of the light of His countenance. They are ready to say to themselves, *If God loves me, why doesn't He owe me more comfort? Why does He see me in such darkness and not comfort me?*

If their happiness throughout all eternity will be so great, of how little consequence is their condition for that short moment they continue in this world! What if they are in the dark, what if they walk in darkness and are exercised with great trouble! How little difference will it make, though it be cast into the scales, when weighed against that far more exceeding and eternal weight of glory! It will prove lighter than vanity. If God gives eternal happiness to them, that is evident proof of His love, and all the darkness and sorrow they can meet with in this world are not worthy to be mentioned. All this darkness, however long it continues, vanishes into nothing if we compare it with future glory.

Reflection

What questions do you have for God?
Are you asking them?
How might the perspective of heavenly glory help to ease your pain, darkness, and sorrow here on earth?

Seek Clean Hands and a Pure Heart

"Blessed are the pure in heart, for they shall see God."

Matthew 5:8

Y ou must be pure in heart and clean in hands. Only the pure in heart will see God. Those who will ascend into God's holy hill are those who have pure hearts and clean hands (Ps. 24:3-4). You must hate and abhor all sin, and allow none in your life. Sin must become to you a great burden. You must loathe yourself, and fight and strive against it, to purge yourself more and more from it, striving more and more to mortify sin, earnestly desiring and seeking to be more holy, more conformed to the will of God, and to walk in ways appropriate for a Christian.

Reflection

Which sins do you find most difficult to battle?

How might you enlist more help from God in becoming more holy and more conformed to His will?

Heaven: A Valuable Treasure

"The kingdom of heaven is like treasure
hidden in a field, which a man found and hid;
and for joy over it he goes and sells all that
he has and buys that field."

Matthew 13:44

Heaven must be to you like the treasure hidden in a field; or like the pearl of great price. If you would have heaven, you must take it as your whole portion. You must in your heart part with all other things for it, and you must continue to part with other things whenever they stand in the way of your getting forward toward heaven. If you would have heaven, you must sell your worldly profit and your credit, the goodwill of your neighbors, your worldly pleasures and conveniences, and whatever stands in your way. Many people flatter themselves that they will obtain heaven without this and think they have a right to heaven, although they were never brought to this. They are sure to find themselves disappointed.

Reflection

How seriously are
you pursuing
heaven?

What might be
standing in your
way of becoming
who God calls you
to be in light of
your eternal
standing with Him?

Choose the Straight and Narrow

"Enter by the narrow gate; for wide is the gate and broad is the way that leads to destruction."

Matthew 7:13

Y ou must never expect to go to heaven by any other than a straight and narrow way. Some people who are not walking in a narrow way expect to get to heaven. The way they are walking is a way of indulging their ease and disregarding the hard and difficult parts of religion. It is not the ways of self-denial, toil, and laboriousness. They walk in a broad way, a way wherein they are not pinched, but can go on without labor, without watchfulness, without bearing the cross. But such people as these—let their hopes be what they may, their profession what it may, and their pretenses toward experiences be what they may—are not likely to get to heaven.

To some people, the way that the Scriptures has laid out is too narrow and straight. Therefore they are endeavoring to get to heaven in a broad way. It is in vain, however, for you to contrive this. If you can find any way of getting to heaven that is not a straight and narrow way, it will be a way that you first invented. If you go that way, you must go in the way of the footsteps of the flock. If you would go to heaven, you must be content to go there in the way of self-denial and sufferings. You must be willing to take up the cross daily and follow Christ, and through much tribulation enter into the kingdom of heaven.

Reflection

What kinds of ways are people inventing in their attempts to reach heaven?

How can a Christian lovingly share the message of this reading without coming across as critical and judgmental of other people's spiritualities?

Love Each Other

"This commandment we have from Him: that
he who loves God must love his brother also."

1 John 4:21

W hat great love God has bestowed on you
in choosing you for such unspeakable
blessedness before the foundation of the
world. How wonderful was the love of God in giving His
Son to purchase this blessedness for you. How wonderful
was the love of the Son of God in shedding His blood to
purchase such glory for you! How ought you therefore
to live for Gods glory! Let me therefore beseech, by those
great mercies of God, that you give yourself up as a living
sacrifice, holy and acceptable to God, which is your
reasonable service. Do not be slothful in business, but
be fervent in spirit, serving the Lord. Give the utmost
diligence so that you may keep all the commandments
of God. Study that you may prove what is the good,
acceptable, and perfect will of God. Study so that in all
things you may be found approved.

Recognizing how much God has loved you, see that
you love one another. Let love be without false pretense.
Be kindly affectionate one with another with brotherly
love. Be of the same mind one toward another, in honor
preferring one another. Have fervent love among your-

selves. Realizing that God has mercy on you, be merciful as your Father in heaven is merciful. Don't just focus on your own things. Be compassionate, courteous, ready to share, and willing to communicate. Be kind one to another, tenderhearted, forgiving one another. Such things as these become those saints who are the heirs of the glory.

Reflection

How well are you succeeding in areas such as these?
What changes might you need to make in order to reflect the love of Jesus even more to people around you?

Live as a Redeemed Person

"Both the earth and the works that are in it will be burned up. Therefore, since all these things will be dissolved, what manner of persons ought you to be in holy conduct and godliness?"

2 Peter 3:10–11

God has redeemed you out of the world, therefore do not live as though you had your portion in this life. Live as pilgrims and strangers, as those who are not at home, as fellow citizens with the saints and of the household of God. Don't be conformed to this world, but be transformed by the renewing of your mind (Rom. 12:2). How dishonorable will it be to you, since God had so advanced and entitled you to such glory, to set your heart on the dust of the earth. How you dishonor the grace of God, which has given you such blessedness.

Why will you dishonor the blessedness that God has given by not setting your heart on it, by setting your heart so much on the world!

Reflection

What does it mean to "dishonor God" and His grace?

Why is it so tempting to set our hearts on earth and what it offers rather than looking toward heaven?

Live a Life Worthy of Christ

"Walk worthy of the Lord, fully pleasing
Him, being fruitful in every good work and
increasing in the knowledge of God."

Colossians 1:10

Consider what a vast difference God has made between you and other people, how vastly different your relative state is from theirs, how much more God has done for you than for them. Seek therefore those things that are above, where God is. Will it not he a shame if a person who is entitled to such glory behaves no better than a child of the Devil?

Walk worthy of the vocation to which you are called. Manifest more love, more meekness, and more humility, with all lowliness and meekness, with long-suffering, forbearing one another in love. Walk worthy of the Lord to all people, "strengthened with all might, according to His glorious power, for all patience and long-suffering" (Col. 1:11). Let your light so shine before men that they will see your good works and glorify your Father, who is in heaven (Matt. 5:16).

Seeing that God has given you so much, God and people may well expect that you should be greatly distinguished in your life from other people.

Reflection

Why is it so important for Christians to "walk worthy" of the Lord?

What happens when they don't do this?

Think about what other people see when they watch and listen to you.

Why God Chooses Us

> "Just as He chose us in Him before the foundation of the world, that we should be holy and without blame before Him in love, having predestined us to adoption as sons by Jesus Christ to Himself, according to the good pleasure of His will."
>
> Ephesians 1:4-5

God does not choose people because they are excellent; He makes them excellent because He has chosen them. It is not because God considers them to be holy that He chooses them; He chooses them so that they might be holy. God does not choose them from the foresight of any respect they will have toward Him. God does not choose people and set His care on them because they love Him, but because He first loved us: "In this is love, not that we loved God, but that He loved us and sent His Son to be the propitiation for our sins" (1 John 4:10). "We love Him because He first loved us" (1 John 4:19).

People do good works because God has chosen them: "You did not choose Me, but I chose you and appointed you that you should go and bear fruit, and that your fruit should remain, that whatever you ask the Father in My name He may give you" (John 15:16).

Reflection

Ask God to show
you what fruit He
wants you to
produce today.
Especially pay
attention to
holiness—any areas
of sin in your life.

Unity among Christians

"I . . . beseech you to walk worthy of the calling
with which you were called, with all lowliness
and gentleness, with long-suffering, bearing
with one another in love, endeavoring to keep
the unity of the Spirit in the bond of peace."

Ephesians 4:1–3

C hristians are all of one kindred. They have a
relationship with other Christians that they do
not have with the rest of the world, being of a
distinct race from them but of the same race one with
another. They are all descended from the same progenitors;
they are the children of the same universal church of God;
they are all the children of Abraham; they are the seed of
Jesus Christ; they are the offspring of God. And they are
yet much more alike than their being of the same race orig-
inally argues them to be: They are also immediately the
children of the same Father. God has begotten all of them
by the same Word and Spirit. They are all of one family
and should therefore love as brethren. "Finally, all of you
be of one mind, having compassion for one another; love
as brothers, be tenderhearted, be courteous" (1 Peter 3:8).

It is very unbecoming for those who are God's offspring
to entertain a spirit of hatred and ill will one toward another. It is very unbecoming to be backward in helping and
assisting one another, and supplying each other's wants,
and even worse to contrive and seek one another's hurt, to
be revengeful one toward another.

Reflection

What causes so much discord among believers?

Is there anyone in your life whom you have tried to hurt?

If so, how might God want you to respond to this person?

What can you do today to promote unity among believers, especially people close to you?

Honor Your Great God

"You know how we exhorted, and comforted,
and charged every one of you, as a father
does his own children, that you would walk
worthy of God who calls you into His own
kingdom and glory."

1 Thessalonians 2:11–12

L et Christians take heed to walk in ways that will not dishonor their pedigree. You are of a very honorable race, more honorable by far than if you were the offspring of kings and had royal blood in your veins. You are a heavenly offspring, the seed of Jesus Christ, the children of God. Those who are of noble race are prone to value themselves highly based on the honor of their families; to dwell on their titles, their coats of arms, and their ensigns of honor; and to recount the exploits of their illustrious forefathers. How much more careful should you be of the honor of your lineage, that you in nothing behave yourself unworthy of the great God, the eternal and omnipotent King of heaven and earth whose offspring you are!

Many things are morally low and too mean for such as you. These include giving way to earthly mindedness, a groveling like moles in the earth, allowing your soul to cleave to earthly things that ought to be neglected and despised by those who are of heavenly descent, indulging in the lusts of the flesh, allowing the soul to be immersed in filth, being taken up with mean and unworthy delights common to the beasts, being intemperate in the gratification of any carnal appetite whatsoever, or being much concerned about earthly honor. It is surely a disgrace for those who are accounted to God for a generation to care whether they are accounted great on this dunghill. It is unworthy of your noble descent to be governed by your passions. You should be guided by higher principles of reason, virtue, and a universal respect of God's glory and honor.

Reflection

Write down some practical ways in which this reading applies to your life.

Why is it so difficult to honor God in all ways these days?

In which particular area do you find this hard to do?

How does a person "respect" God's glory and honor?

Pursue God and His Ways

"Let all those who seek You rejoice and he
glad in You; and let those who love Your
salvation say continually, 'Let God be
magnified!'"

Psalm 70:4

C hristians should seek after spiritual wisdom
and knowledge of the most worthy and noble
truths. They should seek more and more an
acquaintance with God, and to be assimilated to Him—
their great progenitor, their immediate Father—that they
may have the image of His excellent and divine perfections.
They should endeavor to act like God, wherein they are
capable of imitating Him. They should seek heavenly
mindedness: the noble appetites after heavenly and
spiritual enjoyments, a noble ambition after heavenly
glory, a contempt of the trifles and mean things of this
world.

Christians should seek after those delights and sat-
isfactions that can he enjoyed by none but heavenly
minds. They should exercise a spirit of true, universal
love and confidence, and Christian compassion. They
should pay much attention to devotion and divine contemplation.

Reflection

How "heavenly minded" are you?

To what extent do you pursue God and contemplate who He is and His Word?

What is the relationship between "divine contemplation" and godly actions?

Honor Awaits True Believers

"When Christ who is our life appears, then
you also will appear with Him in glory."

Colossians 3:4

T rue Christians will be advanced to honors far above those of earthly kings. They will have a vastly higher dignity than any princes. If these princes are nobly descended, it is not nearly so great an honor as to he the sons of God. If people are nobly educated, and have princely qualifications, these qualifications are not nearly so honorable as those with which God endows His saints, whose minds He fills with divine knowledge and to whom He gives true and perfect holiness. Princes appear honorable from their outward honor and dignity, their royal robes, their stately palaces, and their splendid possessions. But these are not nearly as honorable as the white robes with which the saints will appear in heaven, with which they "will shine forth as the sun in the kingdom of their Father" (Matt. 13:43).

What is a king's palace compared to the mansions in heaven that Christ prepares for His saints? The honor of the creature consists in likeness and nearness to the Creator in heaven. The saints will be like Him, for they will see Him as He is. They wall be most near to Him and will enjoy a most intimate fellowship.

Reflection

How might this
perspective
influence the
manner in which
you face your
hardships?
Affect your level of
joy and hope?

Christ's Sufficiency

"In Him we have redemption through His blood, the forgiveness of sins, according to the riches of His grace which He made to abound toward us in all wisdom and prudence."

Ephesians 1:7–8

Christ is at all times equally sufficient for the office He has undertaken. He undertook the office from eternity, and He was sufficient for it from eternity. He has been exercising His office since the fall of man and remains equally sufficient throughout all ages. His power, wisdom, love, excellency, and worthiness are at all times equally sufficient for the salvation of sinners and for the upholding and glorifying of believers. He is forever able to save because He lives forever. His life is endless and unchangeable. He is made not after the law of a carnal commandment, but after the power of an endless life (Heb. 7:16). He is at all times equally accepted as a Mediator in the sight of the Father, who is always pleased with Him. The sacrifice that He has offered, and the righteousness that He has performed, is at all times equally sufficient. His blood is as sufficient to cleanse away sin now as when it was warm from His wounds.

Reflection

Why is the
sufficiency of Jesus
Christ so
important?

He is unchangeable
in upholding and
preserving those
who are His, but
how does that
commitment relate
to our joy and hope?

Give Your Heart Sacrificially to God

"I beseech you therefore, brethren, by the
mercies of God, that you present your bodies
a living sacrifice, holy, acceptable to God,
which is your reasonable service."

Romans 12:1

The Christian gives himself to God freely,
heartily. He desires to be God's, to belong to
no other. He gives all the faculties of his soul
to God. He gives God his heart and offers it to God as a
sacrifice in two ways.

The first is when the heart is broken for sin. A sacrifice,
before it can be offered, must be wounded and slain. The
heart of a true Christian is first wounded by a sense of
sin—its great evil and danger—and is slain with godly
sorrow and true repentance. When the heart truly re-
pents, it dies to sin. Repentance is compared to a death
in the Word of God:

*Knowing this, that our old man was crucified with
Him, that the body of sin might be done away with, that
we should no longer be slaves of sin. For he who has died
has been freed from sin. Now if we died with Christ, we
believe that we shall also live with Him ... Likewise you
also, reckon yourselves to be dead indeed to sin, but alive
to God in Christ Jesus our Lord. (Rom. 6:6-8, 11)*

Christ, when He was offered, was offered broken on

the cross. So there is some likeness to this. When a soul is converted, the heart is offered to God slain and broken. Psalm 51:17 reads, "The sacrifices of God are a broken spirit, a broken and a contrite heart—these, O God, You will not despise."

Reflection

What does it mean to offer your heart sacrificially to God?

Is your heart wounded by sin, causing you to repent of your sinfulness and ask God to help you?

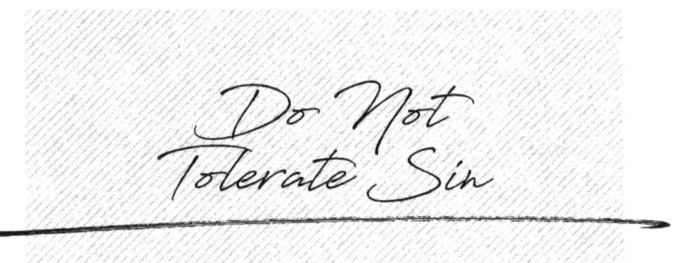

Do Not Tolerate Sin

"Abstain from every form of evil."

1 Thessalonians 5:22

Let all who profess to he Christians take heed that they don't defile themselves and profane their sacred character. There was great strictness required of old of the priests, lest they should defile themselves and profane their office, and it was regarded as a dreadful thing to profane it. The holy God threatened in the New Testament, "If anyone defiles the temple of God, God will destroy him" (1 Cor. 3:17). As Christians are here called the "temple of God," so it is said, in 1 Peter 2:5, that they are "a spiritual house, a holy priesthood."

Avoid committing all immoralities or things that have a horrid filthiness in them, things that will dreadfully profane the sacred name by which you are called and the sacred station wherein you are set. Especially take heed of lascivious impurities. Such things were looked on as defiling the holy office of the priesthood of old.

Take heed of every sin. Allowing any sin whatsoever is a dreadful presumption of your holy character.

Reflection

How can a believer today "take heed of every sin" when each of us is bombarded by sinfulness and tempting messages every day?

What can you do to become more sensitive to your sin and its effects?

Offer Yourself to God

"You also, as living stones, are being built up
a spiritual house, a holy priesthood, to offer
up spiritual sacrifices acceptable to God
through Jesus Christ."

1 Peter 2:5

See that you well execute your office. Offer your heart in sacrifice. Get and keep a close relationship with God. Come to Him boldly. Offer up a heart broken for sin; offer it up flaming with love to God. Offer praise to God for His glorious excellency and for His love and mercy. Consider what great things you have to praise God for: the redemption of Jesus Christ, His sufferings, His obedience, and the gift of that holiness.

Do good. Consider it is part of your office to do that for which you are called and anointed, and as a sacrifice well pleasing to God. Pity others in distress and be ready to help one another. God will have mercy and not sacrifice (Hos. 6:6).

Frequently offer up your prayers to God, and see that they are offered on the right altar. Otherwise they will be abominable to God. Offer your hearts to God through Christ. In His name present the sacrifice of praise, obedience, love, and prayer on the golden altar perfumed with the incense of Christ's merits.

Reflection

What is your calling before God?

Why is praise to God so vital to fulfilling our calling?

What did the author mean when he wrote about offering up prayers "on the right altar"?

Be Watchful and Diligent

"Take heed to yourself, and diligently keep
yourself lest you forget the things your eyes
have seen, and lest they depart from your
heart all the days of your life."

Deuteronomy 4:9

God requires of us that we exercise utmost
watchfulness and diligence in His service.
Reason teaches that it is our duty to exercise
the utmost care, that we may know the mind and will of
God, know our duty, and use our utmost diligence in
everything because the service of God is the great business of our lives. It is the work that is the fulfillment of
our beings, and God is worthy that we should serve Him
to the utmost.

This is what God often expressly requires of us. "You
shall diligently keep the commandments of the Lord your
God" (Deut. 6:17). "Keep your heart with all diligence,
for out of it spring the issues of life" (Prov. 4:23). Christ
commanded us to "watch and pray" (Matt. 26:41) and
said, "Take heed to yourselves, lest your hearts be
weighed down with carousing, drunkenness, and cares
of this life" (Luke 21:34).

If we are found in any way evil, it will not excuse us
that we were not aware of it, as long as it is through lack
of that care and watchfulness in us that we ought to have
maintained.

Reflection

What are you doing to "keep your heart" on the right track?

How can Christians encourage "watchfulness" in one another?

Neglecting Prayer

"Yet they say to God, 'Depart from us, for we
do not desire the knowledge of Your ways.
Who is the Almighty, that we should serve
Him? And what profit do we have if we pray
to Him?'"

Job 21:14-15

He who casts off prayer in effect casts off all
the worship of God, of which prayer is the
principal duty. How miserable a saint who is
not a worshipper of God! He who casts off the worship
of God in effect casts off God Himself. Such a person
refuses to own Him or be conversant with Him as His
God because the way in which men own God and are
conversant with Him is by worshipping Him.

How' can von expect to dwell with God forever if
you so neglect and forsake Him here? Neglecting prayer
shows that you don't place your happiness in God, in
nearness to Him and communion with Him. The person
who refuses to visit and converse with a friend, and who
in great measure forsakes the friend when he is abundantly invited and importuned to visit, plainly shows
that he doesn't receive happiness in that friend's company
and conversation.

If this is your situation, how can you expect to receive
happiness for all eternity from being with God and
enjoying holy communion with Him? Let those people
who hope they are converted, who yet have in a great

measure left off the duty of secret prayer and whose manner it is usually to neglect it, to seriously consider these things.

Streams that have no springs to feed them will dry up. Drought and heat consume the snow waters. Although they run plentifully in the spring, when the sun ascends higher with a burning heat, they are gone. The seed that is sown in stony places, though it seems to flourish at first, will wither away as the sun rises with a burning heat. None will bring forth fruit with patience except those whose hearts have become fertile ground.

Reflection

What has happened to you when you stopped praying, or at least neglected your prayer life?

How much do you desire deep communion with God?

Prize Jesus, Our Faithful Savior

"Jesus said to her, 'I am the resurrection and the life. He who believes in Me, though he may die, he shall live.'"

John 11:25

Consider that it is Christ, and He only, who defends you from wrath. He is a safe defense; your defense is a high tower; your city of refuge is impregnable. There is no rock like your rock. There is no one like Christ, "the God of Jeshurun, who rides the heavens to help you, and in His excellency on the clouds. The eternal God is your refuge, and underneath are the everlasting arms" (Deut. 33:26-27). The One in whom you trust is a shield to all who trust in Him (Ps. 18:30).

Oh, prize that Savior who keeps your soul in safety while thousands of others are carried away by the fury of God s anger and are tossed with raging and burning tempests into hell! Oh, how much better is your situation than theirs! And to whom is it owing but to the Lord Jesus Christ? Remember what your situation once was, and what it is now, and prize Jesus Christ.

Let Christians who are in doubts and fears concerning their condition fly to Jesus Christ, who is a hiding place from the wind and a shelter from the tempest.

Reflection

Thank Christ for His salvation, for loving you so much that He will give you eternal life with Him in heaven.

Reflect on His steadfast love for you and His commitment to defend you.

The Best Way to Witness

"See then that you walk circumspectly."

Ephesians 5:15

I f we live in any sinful way, we live in a way whereby God is dishonored. But all believers ought to supremely regard His honor. If everyone would take care to obey God, live justly and holy, walk according to Christian rules, and maintain a strict watch over himself to ensure there is no wicked way in him, would diligently amend whatever is amiss, would avoid every unholy, unchristian, and sinful way—if the practice of all believers was universally appropriate for Christians—how greatly would this glorify God and Jesus Christ! How it would stop the mouths of objectors and opponents! How beautiful and amiable would religion then appear, when exemplified in the lives of Christians—not maimed and mutilated, but whole and entire, in its true shape, having all its parts and its proper beauty!

If those who call themselves Christians thus walked in all the paths of virtue and holiness, it would do more to advance the kingdom of Christ in the world, the conviction of sinners, and the propagation of Christianity among unbelievers than all the sermons in the world.

Reflection

What keeps some
Christians from
living in this way?
In what ways might
you need to change
some things in
order to live a just
and holy life?

Beware the Sin Nature

"For from within, out of the heart of men,
proceed evil thoughts."

Mark 7:21

The heart of man is naturally prone to sin. The weight of the soul is naturally that way, as the stone by its weight tends to go downward. And saints have a great tendency to sin. Although sin is subjugated in them, yet a body of sin and death remains. There are all manner of lusts and corrupt inclinations. Man is so prone to sinful ways that, without maintaining a constant strict watch over himself, nothing else can be expected than that he will walk in some sinful way. Our hearts are so full of sin that they are ready to betray us. Sin is apt to catch us unawares.

Besides this, we continually meet with temptations. We walk in the midst of snares. And the Devil, a subtle adversary, continually watches over us, endeavoring by all manner of wiles and devices to lead us into wrong paths. "I am jealous for you with godly jealousy . . . I fear, lest somehow, as the serpent deceived Eve by his craftiness, so your minds may be corrupted from the simplicity that is in Christ" (2 Cor. 11:2-3). "Be sober, be vigilant; because your adversary the devil walks about like a roaring lion, seeking whom he may devour" (1 Peter 5:8).

Reflection

Why does every
Christian have to he
so careful?

In what ways have
you seen the Devil
work in your life?

In the lives of
people around you?

Christ Will Turn No One Away

"Come to Me, all you who labor and are heavy laden, and I will give you rest."

Matthew 11:28

C hrist's love, compassion, and gracious disposition are such that we may be sure He will receive all who come to Him. If He would not do it, He would fail in His own undertaking, and also break His promise to the Father and to us. His wisdom and faithfulness will not allow that.

Christ is so full of love and kindness that He is disposed to nothing but to receive and defend us if we come to Him. He is exceedingly ready to pity us. His arms are open to receive us. He delights to receive distressed souls that come to Him, and to protect them. He would gather them as a hen gathers her chickens under her wings. He exceedingly rejoices in this work because He delights in acts of love, pity, and mercy.

Reflection

Why do you think so many people are unwilling to turn to Jesus?

In what ways has His love, pity, and mercy touched you?

Do you find it easy to view Him as One who has open arms toward you?

Why or why not?

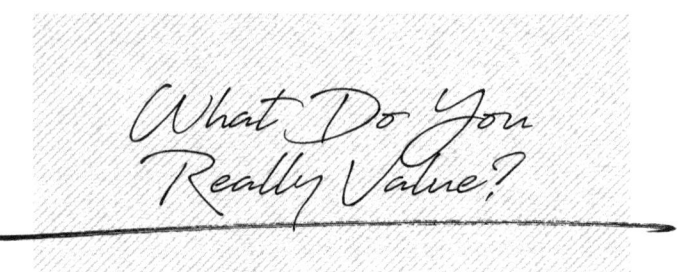

What Do You Really Value?

"My soul thirsts for God, for the living God."

Psalm 42:2

I t is the spirit of a godly man to prefer God to any earthly enjoyments of which he can imagine. He not only prefers God to anything he now possesses, he views nothing any other people possess to be as worthy of admiration. Even if he could have as much worldly prosperity as he desired, the earthly things he could imagine, he values the portion that he has in God incomparably more. He prefers Christ to earthly kingdoms.

Reflection

Do you find it easy to value God more highly than earthly possessions?

Ask God to reveal Himself to you in such a dynamic way that the things of earth will pale in comparison.

All Lusts Are Deceitful

> "All that is in the world—the lust of the flesh, the lust of the eyes, and the pride of life—is not of the Father but is of the world."
>
> 1 John 2:16

The more a man lives in a way of covetousness, or the more inordinately he desires the profits of the world, the more he will excuse himself for doing so and the more he will think that he has a right to those things, cannot do without them, and is excusable for eagerly desiring them if they are necessary. The same might he shown of all the lusts that are in men's hearts. The more they prevail, the more they blind the mind and incline the judgment to approve of them. All lusts are deceitful lusts. "Put off, concerning your former conduct, the old man which grows corrupt according to the deceitful lusts" (Eph. 4:22). Even godly men may for a time be blinded and deluded by a lust, and thereby live in a way that is displeasing to God.

Reflection

Think about why
lusts are deceitful.
What lies do they
encourage you to
believe concerning
yourself, God, and
other people?

Wonderful Benefits of Prayer

"I will call upon the Lord, who is worthy to
be praised."

Psalm 18:3

Consider the great benefits of a constant, diligent, and persevering focus on the duty of prayer. It is one of the greatest and most excellent means of nourishing the new nature, and of causing the soul to flourish and prosper. It is an excellent means of keeping up an acquaintance with God and growing in the knowledge of Him. It is the way to a life of communion with God. It is an excellent means of removing the heart from the world's vanities and causing the mind to be conversant in heaven. It is an excellent preservation from sin and the Devils wiles, and is a powerful antidote against the poison of the old serpent. It is a duty whereby strength is derived from God against the heart's lusts and corruption and the world's snares.

The duty of prayer has a great tendency to keep the soul in a wakeful state, lead us to a strict walk with God and to a life that will be fruitful in good works and cause our light so to shine before other people that they, seeing our good works, will glorify our Father who is in heaven. If the duty of prayer is constantly and diligently attended, it will be a very pleasant duty.

Reflection

How do the benefits of "the duty of prayer" mentioned here relate to your needs?

The needs of other people around you?

Which of prayers benefits do you particularly need right now?

The Effects of Sin on Prayer

"If I regard iniquity in my heart, The Lord
will not hear."

Psalm 66:18

It is the manner of hypocrites, after awhile, to
return to sinful practices that tend to keep them
from praying. While they were under convictions, they reformed their lives and walked carefully. But
as these things die away, their old lusts revive. By degrees, they return like the dog to his vomit. They return
to their sensual, worldly, proud, and contentious practices.

No wonder this makes them forget their prayer
closets. Sinning and praying do not agree well together.

If a man is constant in the duty of secret prayer, it
will tend to restrain him from willful sinning. If he allows
himself to commit sinful practices, they will restrain him
from praying. A man who knows he lives in sin will not
be inclined to come daily into God's presence but will
rather be inclined to flee from His presence, just as Adam,
when he had eaten of the forbidden fruit, ran away from
God and hid among the trees of the garden.

To keep up the duty of prayer after he has let loose
his lusts would tend to disquiet his conscience. It would

give his conscience advantage to testify against him. Therefore hypocrites, as they by degrees admit their wicked practices, exclude prayer.

Why does sin keep people from prayer?
Why is it so important for you to keep your conscience clear before God?

A Just Hatred of Sin

"You have loved righteousness and hated
lawlessness."

Hebrews 1:9

A due sense of the evil of sin, and a just hatred of it, will necessarily cause us to avoid things that expose and lead to sin. If we were duly sensible of sin s dreadful nature, we would have an exceeding dread of it in our spirits. We would hate it worse than death, fear it more than the Devil, and dread it even as we dread damnation. Those things that men exceedingly dread, they naturally shun.

As sin in its own nature is infinitely hateful, so in its natural tendency it is infinitely dreadful. It is the tendency of all sin, eternally, to undo the soul. Every sin naturally carries hell in it! Therefore, we ought to treat all sin as we would treat an infinitely terrible thing. If anyone sins the least sin, that does not necessarily bring eternal ruin with it. This is due to nothing but Gods free grace and mercy to us, and not to the nature and tendency of sin itself. But certainly we ought not to take less care to avoid sin, or all that tends to it, because of the freeness and greatness of Gods mercy to us, through which there is hope of pardon. That would indeed be a most ungrateful and vile abuse of mercy.

If it were made known to us that, if we ever voluntarily committed any particular act of sin, we would be damned without any remedy or escape, wouldn't we exceedingly dread committing such sin? Wouldn't we be very watchful and careful to stand at the greatest distance from that sin and from everything that might expose us to it, from anything that has any tendency to stir up our lusts or betray us to committing such an act of sin?

Reflection

Do you shun all evil?

Which sins do you tend to overlook because you enjoy them?

How do you think God views the willful disobedience of believers?

Beware Temptation

"He who trusts in his own heart is a fool."

Proverbs 28:6

Whoever knows himself is aware of how weak he is and his constant tendency to ran into sin. He who knows how full of corruption his heart is, will he not be very watchful against everything that may lead and expose to sin? Christ directed us, in Matthew 26:41, "Watch and pray, lest you enter into temptation." The reason is added: "The flesh is weak." The person who, in confidence of his own strength, boldly runs the risk of sinning by going into temptation, manifests great presumption, and an insensibility of his own weakness.

Some of the most holy people in the world have been overthrown by such means. So was David; so was Solomon —his wax es turned away his heart. If such persons were this way led into sin, surely that should warn us. "Let him who thinks he stands take heed lest he fall" (1 Cor. 10:12). Such Christians may long withstand temptation and he overcome at last. None are in as much danger as the most bold. Those who are safest are most aware of their own weakness, distrustful of their own hearts, and aware of their continual need of restraining grace.

Reflection

Many Christians today know all about temptation, yet "play with fire." Why?

Which temptations regularly lead you into sin? What can you do to avoid them?

Call on Your Heavenly Father

"Continue earnestly in prayer, being vigilant
in it with thanksgiving."

Colossians 4:2

The spirit of prayer is a holy spirit, a gracious spirit. We read of the spirit of grace and supplication in Zechariah 12:10: "I will pour on the house of David and on the inhabitants of Jerusalem the Spirit of grace and supplication." Whenever there is a true spirit of supplication, there is the spirit of grace. The true spirit of prayer is no other than God's own Spirit dwelling in the hearts of saints. And because this Spirit comes from God, it naturally gravitates toward God in holy breathings and pantings. It naturally leads to God to converse with Him in prayer. Therefore the Spirit is said to make intercession for saints with groanings that cannot be uttered (Rom. 8:26).

The Spirit of God makes intercession for the saints. This Spirit in some respect composes their prayers and leads the saints to pour out their souls before God. John 4:23 says that "the true worshipers will worship the Father in spirit and truth." The truly godly have the spirit of adoption, the spirit of a child, to whom it is natural to go to God and call on Him, crying to Him as to a father.

Reflection

Do you naturally call on God, crying to Him—your heavenly Father?

Why or why not?

Which areas of your life would greatly benefit from such prayers?

Our Future Rewards

"Judge nothing before the time, until the Lord comes, who will both bring to light the hidden things of darkness and reveal the counsels of the hearts. Then each one's praise will come from God."

1 Corinthians 4:5

We are told that every man will be judged according to his works and that Christ keeps a hook of remembrance of the good works of the saints as well as of the sins of the ungodly. However inconsequential and polluted what the saints do is, all the pollution that accompanies it is hidden.

Everything they do for God with sincerity is precious in His eyes. Through His infinite grace, it will not lose its reward or honor. At the day of judgment, saints will receive praise and glory in reward for it. Christ will declare all the good they have done to their honor—what they did secretly, when they did not let their left hand know what their right had done. Then they will receive praise and honor for all their labor, self-denial, and suffering in the cause of Christ.

"God is not unjust to forget your work and labor of love which you have shown toward His name, in that you have ministered to the saints, and do minister" (Heb. 6:10).

Reflection

If you really take
the message of this
reading to heart,
how will you live
differently?

In what ways might
you desire to change
your words,
thoughts, and
actions?

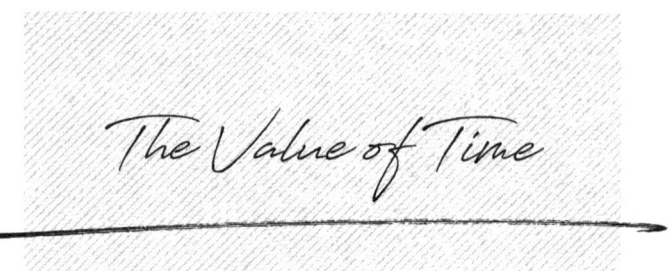

The Value of Time

"What is your life? It is even a vapor that
appears for a little time and then vanishes
away."

James 4:14

The scarcity of any commodity causes people to set a higher value on it, especially if it is necessary and they cannot do without it. Thus when Samaria was besieged by the Syrians, and provisions were exceedingly scarce, "a donkey's head was sold for eighty shekels of silver, and one-fourth of a cab of dove droppings for five shekels of silver" (2 Kings 6:25). So, time is even more to be prized by people because a whole eternity depends on it, yet we have but a little time. "For when a few years are finished, I shall go the way of no return" (Job 16:22). "Now my days are swifter than a runner . . . They pass by like swift ships, like an eagle swooping on its prey" (Job 9:25-26).

It is but as a moment to eternity. Time is so short, and the work that we have to do in it is so great that we have none of it to spare. The work that we have to do to prepare for eternity must be done in time, or it never can be done.

Reflection

What challenges do you face in the use of time?

If you knew that you would die and be in eternity next week, how would you live life differently today?

What keeps you from living that way every day?

A Personal Checklist

"Choose for yourselves this day whom you
will serve."

Joshua 24:15

I nquire whether you have ever come to a determination about religion with respect to the
practice of it, whether you have chosen heaven
with the way to it—the way of obedience and self-denial.
Here I will mention some signs that people halt between
two opinions in this matter.

1. To put off duty until later. When people love to keep
   their duty at a distance, not engaging in it for the
   present, but think of engaging when it will be more
   convenient for them.

2. When persons are strict and conscientious in some
   things, but not universal in their obedience. They do
   some duties, but live in the omission of others. They
   avoid some sins, but allow themselves to sin in other
   ways. They are conscientious with respect to the
   duties of worship (public and private), but not in their
   behavior toward their neighbors. They are not just
   in their dealings, nor conscientious in paying their
   debts, nor do they do to others as they would desire
   people to do to them.

3. If persons sometimes are considerably engaged in religion, but at other times neglect it. Sometimes forming a resolution to be in good earnest, then dropping it again. Sometimes seeming to be really engaged in seeking salvation and earnest in religious duties, but at other times wholly taken up with the things of this world while neglecting religion and omitting religious duties.

4. If people resist their duty whenever any notable difficulty comes in the way, considerably opposed to their interest or inconsistent with ease, convenience, or temporal honor.

Reflection

How does your life stack up against the authors checklist?
If your life reflects spiritual indecision, what do you plan to do about it?

Study God's Word Deeply and Often

"Your word is a lamp to my feet and a light to my path."

Psalm 119:105

I t is true that our hearts are exceedingly deceitful. But God, in His holy Word, has given that light with respect to our duty, which is accommodated to the state of darkness in which we are. So, by thorough care and inquiry, we may know our duty and know whether or not we live in any sinful way. Everyone who has any true love for God and His duty will be glad of assistance in this inquiry.

If we would know whether we live in some sinful way, we should take a great deal of pains to be thoroughly acquainted with the rule. God has given us true and perfect rules by which we ought to walk. And in order that we might be able, notwithstanding our darkness and disadvantages that attend us, to know our duty, He has laid the rules before us abundantly. What a full and abundant revelation of the mind of God have we in the Scriptures! And how plain it is in what relates to practice! How often are rules repeated! In how many various forms are they revealed, that we might the more fully understand them!

Therefore, lest we go in ways displeasing to God, we ought to study diligently the rules God has given us. We ought to read and search the holy Scriptures much, and do it with the goal of knowing the whole of our duty.

Reflection

How does the time a Christian studies the Bible influence the degree to which Gods power can manifest itself through him or her?

How much emphasis do you put on discovering the mind of God revealed in Scripture?

Why do you think many people today no longer believe that the Bible is relevant to their lives?

Be Generous to Those in Need

"If a brother or sister is naked and destitute of daily food, and one of you says to them, 'Depart in peace, be warmed and filled,' but you do not give them the things which are needed for the body, what does it profit? Thus also faith by itself, if it does not have works, is dead."

James 2:15–17

To love our neighbor as ourselves is the sum of the moral law respecting our fellow creatures. To help them and contribute to their relief is the most natural expression of this love. It is vain to pretend to have a spirit of love toward our neighbors when it is grievous to us to part with anything for their help when they are in need. Those who love only in word and tongue, and not in deed, have no love in truth. Any profession without action is a vain pretense. To refuse to give to the needy is unreasonable because we therein do to others contrary to what we would have others do to us in similar circumstances.

Consider how much God has done for us, how greatly He has loved us, and what He has given us when we were so unworthy and when He could have no addition to His happiness by us. Consider that silver, gold, and earthly crowns were in His esteem but insignificant things to give us, and He has therefore given us His own Son. Christ loved and pitied us when we were poor, and He laid out Himself to help, even shedding His own blood for us without complaint.

Considering all these things, what a poor business will it be if those who hope to share these benefits cannot give something for the relief of a poor neighbor without complaint!

Reflection

In what ways are you generous toward other people who are less fortunate than you are?

Ask God to make you even more sensitive to other people who need practical help.

Subject Index

Worldliness

Wrath

If you have enjoyed this book, look out for these other additions to the series for sale online:

The Best of Andrew Murray
The Best of George MacDonald
The Best of Robert Murray McCheyne
The Best of F. B. Meyer
The Best of E. M. Bounds
The Best of Charles Spurgeon
The Best of D. L. Moody

If this book has impacted your life, we would love to hear from you.
Please contact us at info@honorbooks.com